Creating Welcoming Learning Environments

Full details of all our publications can be found on http://www.multilingual-matters.com, or by writing to Multilingual Matters, St Nicholas House, 31–34 High Street, Bristol, BS1 2AW, UK.

Creating Welcoming Learning Environments

Using Creative Arts Methods in Language Classrooms

Edited by
**Jane Andrews and
Maryam Almohammad**

MULTILINGUAL MATTERS
Bristol • Jackson

DOI https://doi.org/10.21832/ANDREW5792
Library of Congress Cataloging in Publication Data
A catalog record for this book is available from the Library of Congress.
Names: Andrews, Jane (Professor of education), editor. | Almohammad, Maryam, editor.
Title: Creating Welcoming Learning Environments: Using Creative Arts Methods in Language Classrooms/Edited by Jane Andrews and Maryam Almohammad.
Description: Bristol, UK; Jackson, TN: Multilingual Matters, 2022. | Includes bibliographical references and index. | Summary: "This book provides practical ideas for how children, young people and parents can feel welcomed and affirmed in their multilingual identities and all learners can feel excited by the linguistic diversity of the world's people. The book will be an invaluable resource for educational practitioners, researchers, trainee teachers and teacher educators"— Provided by publisher.
Identifiers: LCCN 2022003419 (print) | LCCN 2022003420 (ebook) | ISBN 9781788925792 (hardback) | ISBN 9781788925785 (paperback) | ISBN 9781788925815 (epub) | ISBN 9781788925808 (pdf)
Subjects: LCSH: English language—Study and teaching—Foreign speakers. | Creative activities and seat work. | Multilingual education. | Art in education. | Classroom environment.
Classification: LCC PE1128 .C757 2022 (print) | LCC PE1128 (ebook) | DDC 372.6—dc23/eng/20220414 LC record available at https://lccn.loc.gov/2022003419
LC ebook record available at https://lccn.loc.gov/2022003420

British Library Cataloguing in Publication Data
A catalogue entry for this book is available from the British Library.

ISBN-13: 978-1-78892-579-2 (hbk)
ISBN-13: 978-1-78892-578-5 (pbk)

Multilingual Matters
UK: St Nicholas House, 31–34 High Street, Bristol, BS1 2AW, UK.
USA: Ingram, Jackson, TN, USA.

Website: www.multilingual-matters.com
Twitter: Multi_Ling_Mat
Facebook: https://www.facebook.com/multilingualmatters
Blog: www.channelviewpublications.wordpress.com

Copyright © 2022 Jane Andrews, Maryam Almohammad and the authors of individual chapters.

All rights reserved. No part of this work may be reproduced in any form or by any means without permission in writing from the publisher.

The policy of Multilingual Matters/Channel View Publications is to use papers that are natural, renewable and recyclable products, made from wood grown in sustainable forests. In the manufacturing process of our books, and to further support our policy, preference is given to printers that have FSC and PEFC Chain of Custody certification. The FSC and/or PEFC logos will appear on those books where full certification has been granted to the printer concerned.

Typeset by SAN Publishing Services.
Printed and bound in the UK by the CPI Books Group Ltd.

Contents

	Contributors	vii
1	Introduction: Connecting Creative Arts Approaches With Supporting Children and Young People Developing English as an Additional Language *Jane Andrews and Maryam Almohammad*	1
2	The Well in Welcoming *Alison Phipps*	10
3	Working With Community Filmmaking in Multilingual and Intercultural Language Education *Maryam Almohammad*	23
3.1	Celebration Through Film *Gemma Sharland*	36
3.2	A Filmmaking Project *Alicja Lievaart*	38
4	Creating Together – The Role of Creative Arts in an ESOL Classroom *Lyn Ma*	42
4.1	Working With Children's Needs and Preferences Using Creative Techniques *Su Tippett*	58
4.2	Assessing Children's Language Using Creative Techniques *Judith Prosser*	62
4.3	Building Cohesion in School Through Crafting *Karen Thomas and Rebecca Reeve*	65
5	Adinkra Creative Links – Music and Textiles in Welcoming Learning Environments *Gameli Tordzro and Naa Densua Tordzro*	68
5.1	Working With Adinkra Symbols and Printing – Unlocking Creativity in Children *Alison Grotzke*	83

5.2	A School Radio Station *Dominique Moore*	87
5.3	Singing Songs From Jamaica in Early Years Settings and Primary Schools in South Gloucestershire *Lois Francis*	91
5.4	Audio in School – School Languages on the Tannoy System *Judith Prosser*	95
6	A Conversation With Tawona Sitholé, Poet and Musician	98
6.1	Creative Arts Processes for Working With EAL Children *Anna Comfort*	114
6.2	GCSE English, Using Poetry Written in Students' First Languages *Dominique Moore*	121
7	The Welcome Banner: Cultural Exchange Through Creative Collaboration *Luci Gorell Barnes*	125
8	Creativity, Collaboration and Ways Forward for EAL Learners *Jean Conteh*	135
	Afterword: Summary of Ideas for Practice *Jane Andrews and Maryam Almohammad*	144
	Index	145

Contributors

Maryam Almohammad is an educator in language and intercultural communication at the Institute for Language Education, the Moray House School of Education and Sport, University of Edinburgh, UK. Her research and teaching focus on interculturality, intercultural citizenship, language, identities, art, creativity and power. She draws upon ethnographic research, sociological theories of practice, art-based methods and uses critical, postmodernist and posthumanist approaches.

Jane Andrews is a Professor of Education at the Department of Education & Childhood at the University of the West of England, UK. Jane is also a joint programme leader of the Professional Doctorate in Education (EdD) and contributes to teaching on the BA (Hons) Early Childhood. Jane has research and teaching interests in languages and education and in particular children developing English as an Additional Language. Previous research projects have included Researching Multilingually at Borders, funded by the Arts & Humanities Research Council and the Home-School Knowledge Exchange project, funded by the Economic and Social Research Council.

Anna Comfort is currently working as a Key Stage 1 class teacher and EAL coordinator at St. Michael's on The Mount Primary School that lies in the heart of Bristol. She has taught a diverse range of children in inner city schools and has a real passion for working particularly with bilingual learners. In 2011, Anna took a sabbatical in India where she worked for a local charity delivering teacher training workshops designed to help train and support primary school teachers in schools in Panjim Goa. Prior to this, Anna worked as an ESOL tutor for three years teaching both refugees and asylum seekers in Leeds and Bristol.

Jean Conteh worked for more than 40 years in multilingual settings as a primary teacher, teacher-educator and researcher. She has published widely in the field for a range of audiences; her book for teachers, *The EAL Teaching Book* (Sage), now in its third edition, has become a standard text for schools and teacher education. For 12 years, she ran a bilingual Saturday School in Bradford with two of her former students, and she researched and wrote extensively about the children who attended, their families and their links with their mainstream schools. Now retired, she lives in Northumberland and still writes and gives the occasional talk.

Lois Francis is a qualified teacher with an MA degree in Education. She has more than 20 years of experience working in settings, schools and local authorities in providing support for Black and Asian Minority Ethnic Pupils (BAME) including those with English as an Additional Language (EAL). The emphasis of her work is on closing the educational gap for BAME and EAL pupils. Her knowledge and expertise covers such areas as EAL pedagogy; support for African Caribbean pupils; raising attainment for Gypsy Roma and Traveller children; working with settings and schools to promote cultural diversity and to develop positive relationships with families and communities.

Luci Gorell Barnes began her professional life in the world of physical theatre but migrated to the realm of visual arts. Her work revolves around themes of childhood, isolation and belonging, and she writes, and makes books, maps and animated films to explore these ideas. Her participatory practice is concerned with those who find themselves on the margins for one reason or another, and she develops responsive processes that help people to think imaginatively with themselves and others. Her creative collaborations contribute to a range of disciplines that includes academic research, family support, health services and education.

Alison Grotzke turned her sights on a new career and a fresh challenge as a teaching assistant after being made redundant in 2012 from a financial role of 22 years. She currently works at Wheatfield Primary School in Bradley Stoke, Bristol, as a Year 1 teaching assistant and also dedicates support towards those children with EAL across the school. Her intervention focuses mainly on those who need the basics so that they can interact socially, become more independent and participate with confidence in school life. She seeks to use creativity where possible with the children, as she sells her own artwork, and finds that learners respond positively to this approach.

Alicja Lievaart, MA in Applied Linguistics and Teaching English as a Second Language, Teacher of The Deaf MA, started teaching English in Poland more than 15 years ago and is currently the English Lead at Elmfield School for Deaf Children in Bristol. Being a non-native speaker of English and having worked at various provisions including language schools, special and mainstream schools both in the UK and in Poland, she gives her a unique perspective on teaching English to EAL children. Her classroom practice based on the EAL methodology combined with a creative approach to the English curriculum has been a great success among her students.

Dominique Moore – I benefit from being bilingual and being married to a polyglot. I love listening to, and dancing to, a wide range of music and enjoy literature and cuisines from around the world. I have worked in the civil service and industry. I have had the pleasure of teaching and providing support in primary and secondary schools as a class teacher and as an advisory teacher with two local authority Ethnic Minority Achievement Services. I have benefited from working in schools with diverse school populations and always sought to positively reflect the pupils' heritages in the curriculum resources I used.

Lyn Ma has been teaching for more than 25 years. She has taught internationally and has been a secondary school teacher in an English comprehensive school. She is currently a senior lecturer in ESOL and teaches ESOL at Glasgow Clyde College, Anniesland Campus. She has special responsibility for co-ordinating and teaching on the 16+ ESOL programme; this programme is unique in Scotland as it is specifically for young asylum seekers and refugees between the ages of 16 and 19, many of whom are here alone. She has run the 16+ programme since 2009. She particularly enjoys using creative arts in her teaching.

Alison Phipps is UNESCO Chair in Refugee Integration through Languages and the Arts at the University of Glasgow and Professor of Languages and Intercultural Studies. She was De Carle Fellow at Otago University in 2019, Distinguished Visiting Professor at the Waikato University, Aotearoa New Zealand 2013–2016, Thinker in Residence at the EU Hawke Centre, University of South Australia in 2016, Visiting Professor at Auckland University of Technology and Principal Investigator for AHRC Large Grant 'Researching Multilingually at the Borders of Language, the Body, Law and the State'. She is now co-director of the Global Challenge Research Fund South-South Migration Hub, MIDEQ and for the £2 Million Cultures of Sustainable Peace. She is an academic, activist and published poet.

Judith Prosser holds a BEd from Bristol Polytechnic (now UWE) and has taught in Bristol schools for more than 25 years. In her early career, she taught in mixed first language infant classes in Sudan and Oman, and it is this experience that has shaped her approach to EAL. After teaching for many years in both working-class and middle-class primary schools in Bristol, Judith changed direction, and after CELTA training, she focused on EAL teaching at secondary level, in two quite different schools. Making use of her primary training and experience, Judith uses a creative approach to EAL and pupil engagement.

Rebecca Reeves studied English at Leeds University before spending time working abroad, first with people with a learning disability, and then teaching English. She moved to Portsmouth in 1997 and continued to teach English as a Foreign Language there before doing a PGCE at Chichester University. Becca's teaching career has spanned more than three decades and, although specialising in Key Stage 2, has included work across all age groups. She now works in Miltoncross as an EFL teacher and EMA coordinator. Becca has a passion to support refugees and asylum seekers, working with young unaccompanied asylum seekers in particular.

Gemma Sharland was, at the time of writing, an Inclusion Leader, Special Educational Needs Coordinator and teacher in the primary age range. Throughout her career, she has supported many children who were at various stages of learning the English language. Gemma now supports Young Carers in the Bristol area and brings her passion for inclusivity, diversity and supporting young people for whom English is an Additional Language to her new role.

Tawona Sitholé – better known as Ganyamatope (my ancestral family name) – my heritage inspires me to make connections with other people through creativity, and the natural outlook to learn. I am widely published as a poet and playwright and as a short story author. A storyteller and musician, I am co-founder of Seeds of Thought, a non-funded arts group. I am currently UNESCO artist-in-residence at the University of Glasgow, with research and teaching roles in the school of education and medical school. Other educational roles are with Glasgow School of Art, University of the West of Scotland, University of Stirling and Newcastle University and Scottish Book Trust.

Karen Thomas has taught in both junior and secondary schools, as well as working extensively in the adult and community sector, and is now the Manager and Lead Adviser of Portsmouth's Ethnic Minority Achievement Service. She has a Master's in Education from Sussex University, with a particular emphasis on Assessment for Learning and EAL, as well as a Postgraduate Certificate in Practice and Pedagogy, focusing on the teaching of English as an Additional Language. Karen lectures on local ITT courses and trains and supports staff in Portsmouth schools. She also manages the DfE-funded 'Starting Out' provision for unaccompanied asylum-seeking children.

Su Tippett comes from a background of 20 years' Design, Print and Account Management experience. More recently in 2002, she qualified as a Childminder and then as a Level 3 SEN Teaching Assistant in 2008. Su has supported SEN students across schools both in Bristol and South Gloucestershire. She has worked with a wide range of students with complex needs including Global Delay, ADHD, Autism and Visual Impairments, and more latterly EAL and SEN. She delivers this support through a holistic, sensory approach which works to create a nurturing and enjoyable learning environment that all young people can engage and participate in.

Gameli Tordzro is a multiple-arts practitioner, educator and artistic researcher. He is an Artist in Residence and lecturer with the UNESCO Chair on Refugee Integration Through Languages and The Arts (UNESCO RILA), and Research Associate of The UKRI GCRF South-South Migration, Inequality and Development Hub (MIDEQ), at the University of Glasgow School of Education. He is a member of the UNESCO Arts Lab, and the Society for Artistic Research. He researches in creative arts and translating cultures, arts, indigenous language in education and development, African literature, story and storytelling. He is the founder/composer of Ha Orchestra and editor of AdinkraLinks Network. Twitter: @GTordzro Website: www.gameli.co.uk

Naa Densua Tordzro is a research assistant at on the South-South Migration Inequality and Development Hub (MiDEQ Hub) at the University of Glasgow where she has just completed her MPhil research student in the School of Education. She holds a BA in Fashion Technology from the Heriot Watt University in Galashiels, Scotland. She is Ghanaian, a fashion designer, dressmaker and African (Ga) music composer and singer with knowledge and research interest in ancient West African Adinkra symbols that were printed on traditional fabrics. Her current research focus is on decolonising textiles and fashion education in the contexts of the global south. Naa Densua has been awarded a James McCune Smith scholarship to complete her doctoral study in the University of Glasgow School of Modern Languages. Twitter @AfricanChill Website: http://www.naadensua.com/

1 Introduction: Connecting Creative Arts Approaches With Supporting Children and Young People Developing English as an Additional Language

Jane Andrews and Maryam Almohammad

1 Why Creative Arts Approaches?

Over many years educators have expressed their commitment to drawing on and embedding the arts in education. Nutbrown (2013: 3) explains this commitment as coming from the fact that 'human beings need the arts for holistic development'. Sometime earlier, Rubens and Newland (1989: 5) noted the 'equally important function of Art as an expressive discipline with its own traditions, language and values, capable of enriching all environments, societies, cultures and individuals'. The arts as a contributor to human development and as a language are central to the ideas and practical activities presented in this book which brings together the opportunities provided by creative arts in all their guises with approaches to teaching and learning in mainstream schools and colleges where children and young people are developing their skills in English as an Additional Language (henceforth EAL) and are learning alongside their peers who may also be multilingual speakers, as well as monolingual English speakers. The creative arts approaches explored in the book include making music, singing, drama and performing, printing, collage, drawing, writing poetry, filmmaking and making embroidery.

The book includes both longer chapters (3–7) which set out ideas and principles for working with particular arts-based approaches and also shorter chapters (3.1, 3.2, 4.1, 4.2, 4.3, 5.1, 5.2, 5.3, 5.4, 6.1 and 6.2) where education practitioners (including teaching assistants, teachers and advisory teachers) recount how they worked with an approach and implemented it in their educational setting. The longer chapters set out some principles for a particular way of working with one or more art forms (film, collage, Adinkra symbols and music, the spoken word and embroidery). These chapters contain references intended to take readers further in their exploration of these ideas.

The shorter chapters, on the other hand, are designed to enable readers to learn from a tried and tested activity, used in an educational setting (in England), and to be inspired to transform and adapt it to their own teaching context. The settings in which practitioners developed the activities included primary schools (ages 4–11 in England), secondary schools (ages 12–16 or 18), a school for young people with Special Educational Needs, many of whom were multilingual speakers (in this case for 7–16 year olds) and a school for deaf pupils (from nursery age up to 18). Not all of the activities in the book were tried with all ages of children and young people; however, the purpose of the book is to open out principles for bringing together creative arts approaches with teaching and learning used to support learners' developing English language skills in mainstream schools or colleges and to provide ideas for readers to adapt and try out in their own settings.

We appreciate and recognise previous work which has explored and reported on ways in which the learning of children and young people developing EAL, or multilingual learners in English-medium educational settings, can be enhanced through the use of the creative arts. Cummins and Early (2011) provide a strong call for educators to recognise that creative arts can provide all learners with access to opportunities for exploring, expressing and enhancing their identities through the production of what they call 'identity texts'. Their book is a model for ours in that it sets out a challenge to educators and then offers a rich selection of chapters, written by practising teachers, illustrating how teaching and learning can be enriched through the authoring by learners of identity texts which are meaningful to them and are also rich opportunities for language development. Their work is located in the Canadian educational context but is offered as a starting point for considering how literacy teaching can be opened out as a way of exploring and expressing multilingual and multiliterate identities.

We can also learn from practice in the UK further education context (16–20 year olds), in Scotland and the work of Frimberger *et al.* (2017) who provide a theoretical and practical consideration of how educators have designed activities to support English language learning and identity enhancement around engaging with artefacts. In their work with unaccompanied asylum-seeking young people, the authors engage with learners on activities such as crafting an identity box, inspired by the artist Joseph Cornell who refers to identity boxes as 'visual poems'. The creation process was seen to allow individual skills and expertise to shine through which might not have been available to the class and their lecturer had the crafting process not be used. Examples included skills in drawing, passions and knowledge about certain sports, and readers can learn more about this work in Chapter 4 of this book.

The question posed as the first subheading in this chapter – Why creative arts approaches? – can be addressed further by reflecting on findings from studies which evidence effective practice for learners developing EAL. In a quantitative study in England of what appears to work in schools which are effective in their work to raise the achievement of learners developing EAL in England, Demie and Lewis (2017) connect a focus on school-based activities which provide recognition of and a celebration of learners' cultural heritage as being a significant factor. The authors also point to 'the effective use of an inclusive curriculum' (2017: 4) as being essential for raising the achievement of learners developing EAL and noted positive outcomes where 'The schools pride themselves on their diversity' (Demie & Lewis, 2017: 8). A further finding in this study was that schools with effective practice were seen to have 'created trust and respect amongst parents and a sense of belonging amongst pupils' (2017: 17). We would suggest that the arts, as visible and audible expressions of identity, can provide the confident and explicit inclusive ethos and sense of belonging which is highlighted by Demie and Lewis' study.

Moving on from the question of 'Why creative arts approaches?' it is important to remain realistic about 'how' an arts-informed approach to teaching and learning can be achieved, given what appears to be a pervasive concern around the world with teachers' workloads and frequently changing educational agendas and curricula and the ever-present focus on testing and assessment. Rubens and Newland (1989) referred to art as a 'tool for learning' and their short book emphasises that, with appropriate support for their skills in working with arts-based methods, mainstream teachers can provide 'the stimulating environment that allows real learning to take place' (Bonner in Rubens & Newland, 1989: 3). Appropriate support is potentially a challenge for teachers looking to develop an arts-based approach to their teaching, in terms of skills, confidence and resourcing. In their writing about creativity, Connery *et al.* (2010) remind us that creativity is rarely achieved through solo endeavour and that collaborative working is a key feature of creative practice.

If we apply this principle of 'creative collaboration', which John-Steiner (2000) has further explored in a separate book, it allows us to open up to working with others to achieve the infusion of creative arts practice into our teaching and learning in schools. Such creative collaborations could come from within the school staff so that teachers from across specialisms create new working partnerships which were not previously explored, e.g. EAL staff working with the staff in the Art Department. Equally, the creative collaboration could involve school staff working with communities outside the school which could include parents and carers with skills to share, volunteers from the community who wish to offer their skills to the school or organisations (which could include galleries, museums, arts/media centres) looking to use their skills in outreach work. In the words of Holzman (2010), there can be no creativity without creating a 'zone of proximal development' (ZPD) using Vygotsky's idea of how learning takes place most effectively. In the context of our book and the ideas shared here, the ZPD could be the space where teaching staff and artist-collaborators work together as well as being the space where teaching staff and learners can collaborate and where learners can collaborate together with peers.

From considering different dimensions of creative collaboration which can take place when arts-based practices are brought together with planning activities for supporting learners developing EAL, it is a natural step to appreciate the language-rich possibilities that are available in a collaborative space. The work of Mercer (2000) in relation to the most productive type of talk in groupwork, in terms of learning, proposes that activities that are carefully planned to allow for what he names 'exploratory talk' are equally effective at promoting thinking and providing rich opportunities for talk. Both of these factors are noted by Cummins (1979, 2008) as important for learners of EAL who need to engage in activities which promote their learning of the curriculum and of the language that the curriculum is delivered in. Cummins expresses this challenge as being one where learners take part in learning activities that are at an appropriate level of cognitive demand (that is, age appropriate and neither too challenging nor too easy) and also context-embedded so that there is a support for the learner in terms of the new language to be encountered. We suggest that that the creative work set out in this book illustrates how collaborative, arts-based work has a strong role to play in the language development of EAL learners.

2 Breadth of EAL Teachers' Work – The Three Levels of Whole School, Whole Class and Working One-to-One

A recent guidance document produced by the UK-based National Association for Language Development in the Curriculum (Bellsham-Revell & Nancarrow, 2019) outlines the roles and responsibilities for school-based EAL coordinators. The document illustrates the breadth and complexity of an EAL professional's role. We suggest that this is not only a challenge but also, as this book demonstrates, a great opportunity to influence practice on many levels in an educational setting and have an impact on children's and young people's experiences. The teachers who are writing in this book have introduced innovations in practice at a whole institution level, at a class level and on a one-to-one level when a learner is working with a teacher/lecturer. The whole institution activities included creating displays reported in Chapter 5.1, hosting events such as assemblies including parental and carer involvement reported in Chapter 3.1 and changing the languages used on a whole school tannoy system to communicate daily messages reported in Chapter 5.4. The class-level activities included working with crafting techniques to create a suitcase to introduce yourself to your peers in the context of a secondary school tutor group, as shown in Chapter 4.3. The individual one-to-one level activities included using collage in assessing language skills of learners who were newly arrived in the setting, and possible the country, explored in Chapter 4.2.

3 Background to the Book

This book is an outcome of two research projects: The first was entitled Researching Multilingually at the Borders of the Law, Language, the Body and the State (funded by the Arts and Humanities Research Council, AH/L006936/1) and took place between 2014 and 2017, and the second, which was a follow-on from that project, was entitled Creating Welcoming Learning Environments: Disseminating Arts-Based Approaches to Including all Learners (AH/R004781/1) and ran in the academic year 2017–2018. In the first project, henceforth RM@Borders, multilingualism was explored amongst people experiencing pressure and pain in contexts of migration. The project was created as a multidisciplinary endeavour bringing together creative artists with academics from disciplines such as law, modern languages, language education, counselling psychology, anthropology and applied theatre studies. A key feature of the project was that the arts were conceptualised as a language and were prominent in the research practice and focus from Day 1 of the study. This is notable as it contrasts with work which has involved arts-based collaboration at an end point of the research process for the purpose of, e.g. reaching a wider audience to disseminate research findings. Thus, the arts-based approaches were used in research team discussions of ideas, e.g. using team drama performances informed by team members' metaphors conceptualising ideas being considered at the time. Also arts-based approaches were used in research encounters with participants such as when engaging clients in sites such as an NGO for refugees. Perhaps one of the best examples of the arts-based approach in the project was that one of the publications produced took the form of a colouring book (Al Mousawi-Sitholé & Sitholé, 2017).

The arts-based practices in the RM@Borders project inspired the CWLE project which worked to support a creative collaboration between the RM@Borders creative artists and school-based staff working with children developing EAL. The Creative Artists who worked on both projects were Lyn Ma and Katja Frimberger who worked with crafting techniques and 'visual poetry' (see Chapter 4), Naa Densua Tordzro and Gameli Tordzro who worked with printing on textiles and music making (see Chapter 5) and Alison Phipps and Tawona Sitholé who worked on multilingualism and poetry (see Chapters 2 and 6). Collectively, the research team (Jane Andrews and Maryam Almohammad) and the creative artists sought to work with teaching staff to explore the following research question:

> What activities are devised when creative artists and language education professionals collaborate together in a workshop environment?

In addition to being guided by the research question, the following three guiding principles defined the ethos of the project:

(i) the project would follow cooperative and collaborative lines with expertise from all participants being valued and elicited through professional dialogues;
(ii) experiential learning would inform the practice to be planned and tailored to specific school contexts so that teachers would experience a technique firsthand before engaging in a process of transformation for their context; and
(iii) a decolonising ethos would inform the engagement between researchers, artists and teaching staff so that there would be an active move to avoid any exploitative practices such as school staff being used as guinea pigs for researchers' ideas.

These three guiding principles will be explained in more detail next. The first principle was that the project had a goal of supporting collaboration while at the same time respecting all collaborators' skill sets and expertise. That is to say the project did not conceptualise the artists as having the only valid set of expertise and the teaching staff as being deficient in arts-based expertise. The work of Edge (1992, 2002) has been informative for this purpose in that he offers a conceptualisation of continuing professional development as a process of 'co-operative development'. This means that CPD participants are seen to be learning with and from each other and are not seen in any way to be deficient or lacking in knowledge or understanding of educational processes and practices. We felt that a cooperative development approach to the CWLE project's work would ensure existing pedagogic practices would be valued while opportunities for new transformations of practice could be allowed to be developed.

The second principle informing the project was that there were no 'recipes' for creative arts practice to be implemented in schools and, besides, contextual variations would make it unlikely that activities would function the same in different schools. Instead, it was felt that if teaching staff were to have a hands-on experience of engaging with the arts-based approaches (making music, printing, writing and performing multilingual poetry), they would then be in a position to design their own variations of the activities tailored to their own teaching contexts. The work of Kolb (1984) and his work on experiential learning informed the way we set up in the workshops where creative artists and teaching staff collaborated and experienced activities together.

The third principle informing the project design was a decolonising orientation in the research and its implementation. We learned from the work of Linda Tuhiwai Smith (2012) that research has been practised as an acquisitive process in the past and that the benefits of research have only accrued to researchers and not to those who have experienced the research or who have been the 'objects' of research. Tuhiwai Smith writes as an insider of the indigenous Māori community in New Zealand and her observations about negative experiences of research stem from the experiences of her community who, she says, were 'othered' and misrepresented in research undertaken by outsiders. Tuhiwai Smith states that research with any group in any context has the potential to do harm to those being researched. Her recommendation is that researchers reflect on their own positionality in their research and their goals and methods. She names this process one of 'decolonising methodologies'. In our project, we sought to create open, discursive spaces in which experiences and ideas could be generated and shared but that no one person or group would dominate or dictate the actions of any other group member. This meant, for example, that the workshops to which teaching staff were invited were experiential opportunities rather than a training course.

The way in which these three principles were put into practice is best illustrated by showing (Figure 1.1) an outline for a workshop on the CWLE project.

The outline for the day shows a sequence of activities which allowed for professional expertise and interests to be shared early in the day so that a spirit of co-operation and collaboration could be established from the beginning. The second element of the day prioritised hands-on practice with one or more arts-based techniques, a return to an original meaning of the concept of a workshop. The final part of the day involved planning for future, school-based activities informed by the earlier experiences and interactions on the day.

Workshop outline

Using music and textiles with Naa Densua Tordrzo and Gameli Tordzro

Outline for the day

9am to 10:30	Introductions
	Overview of the Creating Welcoming Learning Environments project
	Sharing of current practices
10:30 to 11:00	Refreshment break
11am to 1pm	Hands-on workshop with Naa Densua Tordrzo and Gameli Tordzro
1pm to 2pm	Lunch break
2pm to 3:30pm	Planning session – how might we adapt ideas encountered in the morning session into our own work with children and young people. How might the project team support you in putting into practice some of these ideas?

Figure 1.1 An outline of a workshop in the CWLE project

4 The Structure of the Book

We end this chapter with an explanation of the sequence and content of the chapters in the book. We also note that during our time working on the CWLE project, we connected up with additional professionals and practices which were relevant to our interests and so these contributors and areas are also represented in the collection. Readers will notice this in the variety and diversity of authorial voices showcased here. A final note needs to go to our approach to ethics and consent. We were guided by the British Educational Research Association Ethical Guidelines (2011, 2018), and consent was sought for participation in all aspects of the research work reported here. Educational professionals writing here have chosen to name themselves and their work settings.

Chapter 2 is written by Alison Phipps whose work on intercultural communication and arts integration in research and language learning has been a great influence on the work in this book. Alison sets us off in a poetic, creative and philosophical mode in her chapter where she considers the origins of words, their meanings and challenges which education systems may inadvertently create for learners who arrive from other countries.

In Chapter 3, Maryam Almohammad explores ideas from published projects which have used filmmaking in language learning in a variety of ways. This work is then followed up with two short chapters (3.1 and 3.2 by Gemma Sharland and

Alicja Lievaart) setting out how they worked with film in a primary school and a secondary school where children who are deaf are educated. In Chapter 4, Lyn Ma explores the principles informing her creative practice using collage and crafting in her work in further education in Scotland with unaccompanied asylum seeker young people. Lyn's work inspired the next three short chapters which took up and adapted the idea of working with collage in the classroom (Chapter 4.1 by Su Tippett, Chapter 4.2 by Judith Prosser and Chapter 4.3 by Karen Thomas and Becca Reeve).

In Chapter 5, Gameli Tordzro and Naa Densua Tordzro present their philosophy and practice working with music and working with textiles and printing, exploring traditional West African Adinkra symbols as tools and inspiration. Naa Densua and Gameli explain their approach as offering 'treasured opportunities' for learning about the origins and meanings of Adinkra symbols which, rather than being a negative experience of cultural appropriation, instead offers opportunities for enriched and contextualised learning. In her chapter (5.1), Alison Grotzke shares her way of working with Adinkra symbols as inspired by Naa Denua and Gameli's work. We then have three chapters exploring music (including singing and DJ-ing) and spoken word (making school announcements in pupils' languages) in the whole school and the classroom context (Chapter 5.2 by Dominique Moore, Chapter 5.3 by Lois Francis and Chapter 5.4 by Judith Prosser).

Chapter 6 takes a different format in that it provides a transcribed and edited conversation between Jane Andrews and Tawona Sitholé, a poet, musician and educator, who also provided inspiration, along with Alison Phipps, in one of the project's workshops. Tawona is experienced in bringing his style of engaging with the spoken word in terms of writing and performing poetry and writing plays into educational settings with learners of different ages. The conversation explores the joys and challenges of such work as well as questions such as where ideas for a poet and playwright come from. In Chapters 6.1 and 6.2, Anna Comfort and Dominique Moore then discuss their practice (in primary and secondary schools) based around performing a play and exploring poetry in different languages.

In Chapter 7, we meet Luci Gorell Barnes who is an artist-in-residence in a primary school which also hosts a children's centre. In her chapter, Luci writes about her creative practices working with parents and children in both indoor and outdoor spaces. As noted by the NALDIC guidance for EAL coordinators (2019) and texts such as Conteh (2015), parental involvement is a vital part of effective educational practice for all learners and that includes learners who are developing EAL. Creative approaches to engaging with children and their parents using the space provided by an allotment and arts-based techniques such as embroidery are discussed in the chapter. Luci's chapter's title refers to 'The Welcome Banner', and the cover for our book shows the co-created welcome banner in all of its beauty.

In Chapter 8, we have invited Jean Conteh to offer a set of reflections on the areas covered throughout, drawing on her experiences and expertise in working with and writing about children, young people, teaching staff and teacher-researchers who work together to continue to develop our collective understandings of the complexities and delights of learning through languages and learning and using languages. We end this edited volume with some key points in an afterword where we share what we have learned about the exciting potential of creating welcoming learning environments in language classrooms and educational settings through bringing in creative arts practices and learners' languages.

References

Al Mousawi-Sitholé, T. and Sitholé, T. (2017) *Broken World Broken Word Colouring Book*. Glasgow: Seeds of Thought.
Bellsham-Revell, A. and Nancarrow, P. (2019) *The EAL Co-ordinator – The First One Hundred Days*. Edinburgh: NALDIC.
BERA (2011, 2018) British Educational Research Association Ethical Guidelines for Educational Research, fourth edition, London. See https://www.bera.ac.uk/researchers-resources/publications/ethicalguidelines-for-educational-research-2018 (accessed February 2022).
Connery, C., John-Steiner, V. and Marjanovic-Shane, A. (eds) (2010) *Vygotsky and Creativity – A Cultural-Historical Approach to Play, Meaning-Making and the Arts*. New York: Peter Language Publishing.
Conteh, J. (2015) *The EAL Teaching Book – Promoting Success for Multilingual Learners*. London: Learning Matters An Imprint of Sage Publications.
Cummins, J. (1979) Cognitive academic language proficiency, linguistic independence, the optimum age question and some other matters. Working papers on bilingualism, No. 19. Toronto: Ontario Institute for Studies in Education.
Cummins, J. (2008) BICS and CALP: Empirical and theoretical status of the distinction in street. In B. Street and N.H. Hornberger (eds) *Encyclopedia of Language and Education, 2nd Edition, Volume 2: Literacy* (pp. 71–83). New York: Springer Science + Business Media LLC.
Cummins, J. and Early, M. (2011) *Identity Texts: The Collaborative Creation of Power in Multilingual Schools*. Stoke-on-Trent: Trentham Books.
Demie, F. and Lewis, K. (2017) Raising achievement of English as additional language pupils in schools: Implications for policy and practice. *Educational Review* 70 (4), 427–446.
Edge, J. (1992) *Co-operative Development Professional Self-development Through Cooperation with Colleagues (Teacher to Teacher)*. Harlow: Longman.
Edge, J. (2002) *Continuing Cooperative Development: A Discourse Framework for Individuals as Colleagues*. Ann Arbor, MI: University of Michigan Press.
Frimberger, K., White, R. and Ma, L. (2017) 'If I didn't know you what would you want me to see?': Poetic mappings in neo-materialist research with young asylum seekers and refugees. *Applied Linguistics Review, Special Issue (Special Issue on Visual Methods)* 9 (2–3), 391–419.
Holzman, L. (2010) Without creating ZPDs there is no creativity. In M.C. Connery, V.P. John–Steiner and A. Marjanovic-Shane (eds) *Vygotsky and Creativity: A Cultural Historical Approach to Play, Meaning Making, and the Arts* (pp. 27–40). New York: Peter Lang.
John-Steiner, V. (2000) *Creative Collaboration*. Oxford: Oxford University Press.
Kolb, D.A. (1984) *Experiential Learning: Experience as the Source of Learning and Development*. Englewood Cliffs, NJ: Prentice Hall.
Mercer, N. (2000) *Words and Minds – How We Use Language to Think Together*. Abingdon: Routledge.
NALDIC (2019) *The EAL Co-ordinator – The First One Hundred Days*. Edinburgh: NALDIC.
Nutbrown, C. (2013) Conceptualising arts-based learning in the early years. *Research Papers in Education* 28 (2), 239–263.
Rubens, M. and Newland, M. (1989) *A Tool for Learning – Some Functions of Art in Primary Education*. Ipswich: Direct Experience.
Tuhiwai Smith, L. (2012) *Decolonising Methodologies – Research and Indigenous Peoples*. London: Zed Books.

2 The Well in Welcoming

Alison Phipps

Hospitable Parts of Speech

Collaborating
Working
Listening
DJ - ing
Sharing
Teaching
Using
Creating
Performing
Assessing
Building
Crafting
Filmmaking
Celebrating
Connecting.

Certain words and their rhythms stand out in the table of contents for this volume. I wonder why. And I'm about to make what may be the mistake of seeing these as verbs and to write about the 'verbing of nouns', the way in the late 1990s in the scholarship in languages and intercultural communication we announced that 'culture was a verb' (Ingold, 1996; Phipps & Gonzalez, 2004). But I hesitate, unsure and knowing that, even as a Professor of Languages, I'm always on unsteady ground when it comes to identifying parts of speech. I am ever a grateful user of grammar books, and my mum.[1] I too am learner of English as I go along with life, just as others are who might not have been born into my specific and situated way of being educated into the world, which begins in the dialects of South Yorkshire Comprehensive Education in the 1980s. Some of these aren't present participles but gerunds, surely, surely?

'The gerund looks exactly the same as a present participle, but it is useful to understand the difference between the two'.

I look at the examples on the website I land on more or less first (see Figure 2.1) – the way you know, when you have lived with certain questions as a researcher, that you are on solid, virtual ground, even if it may not have the word 'Oxford', 'Cambridge', 'Collins', 'Petit Robert' or 'Duden' in front of it. It's instructive, in that it gives me the confidence to be uncertain about these being verbs.

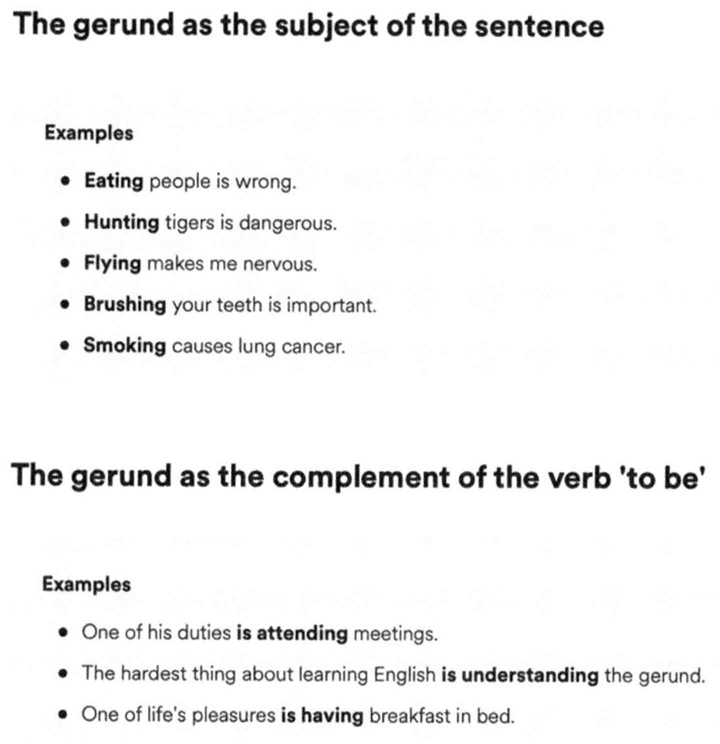

The gerund as the subject of the sentence

Examples

- **Eating** people is wrong.
- **Hunting** tigers is dangerous.
- **Flying** makes me nervous.
- **Brushing** your teeth is important.
- **Smoking** causes lung cancer.

The gerund as the complement of the verb 'to be'

Examples

- One of his duties **is attending** meetings.
- The hardest thing about learning English **is understanding** the gerund.
- One of life's pleasures **is having** breakfast in bed.

Figure 2.1 Screenshot: https://www.ef.com/wwen/english-resources/english-grammar/gerund/

The examples are also instructive, interculturally, as they instantly pitch us up in a moral universe that is constructed out of various elite and colonial narratives. Why on earth would 'eating people is wrong', but the first example for here, I mean, what is it that we are imagining of people who are learning English as an additional, foreign or other language? That they are all tiger hunters? That they may be nervous fliers, that they are unclean and don't brush their teeth, or a health risk like smoking? There are so many other examples that could have been used. Not a welcoming environment this particular, somewhat random learning resource, which I have found in the way many a hassled educator might land on what was resource enough.

I do it all the time when writing titles for talks as do most arts, humanities and social science researchers in the contemporary era. Deconstruction has brought us to a sense of the instability and fluidity of the world, the uncertainty we need to bring to bear critically on our grand narratives and normative certainties; certainties such as 'Tiger hunting is dangerous'. The examples gerunds use as a complement to verbs are equally illuminating. Here is a language written for my work life – 'one of his duties is attending meetings' – for his, of course, as always, read also 'her' or 'their'; 'one of life's pleasures is having breakfast in bed'. We are in a world of bureaucrats and actual beds, and enough food for three meals a day, and an appreciation of leisure time away from the duties of meetings. We are a million miles from the worlds people seeking refuge inhabit day to day.

In my many years of living in a refugee family and in the precarious situation of refugees in third countries, I know that breakfast is a meal you skip because you need the time before the sun is too high to buy or barter for food and water safely. I know that you skip breakfast because two meals a day will mean there is enough for all the extended family and neighbours in the block, or that, within a camp, the designated food distribution and queuing system means that breakfast in bed is no breakfast at all, just time off the interminable queue. 'Hunting tigers may be dangerous' and 'smoking may be bad for your health' but so is being in a refugee camp, and that's the best first option for many. And I know for a fact that the chance of having work, let alone having as one of your 'duties as attending meetings', is the stuff that refugee dreams are made of.

1 The Hardest Thing About Learning English Is….

It's whimsy, and I appreciate it, the example: 'The hardest things about learning English is understanding the gerund'. But it's also fabulously untrue and grounded in the reified realities of linguistics departments in the academy, where the grammars are produced. As Ingold notes, people 'live culturally' rather than inhabiting readily constructed worlds, ones where, for instance, 'Hunting tigers is dangerous'. Culture is not an absolute, any more than language is an absolute, but it is the process by which knowledge is gained. Language is not, for example, the essence of culture; it is the essence of academic culture, and of westernised academic culture and its attendant schooling regimes and entry requirements (Ingold, 1996). There is no universalisable 'hardest thing' about learning, let alone about learning a language. What is relatively easy in one context, maths in a primary school in Eritrea, for instance, might be radically impossible in a school in Glasgow, for the same learner.

Maths. Surely 2 + 2 always = 4.

I am minded of the time I was sitting in glum despair going over maths homework with an English as an Additional Language (EAL) learner and asylum seeker. The maths was easy, but she was completely stuck because of the examples used. They spoke of 'baseball' and 'cricket' games in order to work out mathematical puzzles. She didn't know how to baseball or what cricket was. And felt the question to be impossible. She had been encouraged to take the maths course because 'young people seeking asylum often do well with numbers rather than language-based courses' because it's a more easily understood system and language. This advice was not incorrect, but this welcoming environment of numbers was then rendered unwelcoming not so much by the use of words, but by the normative orientation of the choice of words. The consequences of this for this young person still endure. They are still a maths certificate short of having what they need for entry onto the vocational course of their choice in the medical profession.

If a welcoming environment had been created in their maths lesson, one that equalised the linguistic power by, for once, tipping it in their favour, then a question would ask about numbers of seeds used in a game of ጋጋ and how many you have to have left to win.[2] Speech, of course, as a socially situated activity transitions between social situations, however nuanced, be they those of class or culture, state or system, practice or performance, requires nuance, and hospitality to other ways of describing the world, and other ways of making a world, and care and attention to the ways people can come and go, and stay.

I'm still unsure of my ground here with the grammar in front of my eyes. I call my mum, and she tells me she gave her Fowler's guide to me and I tell her it's stuck in my out-of-bounds-in-a-pandemic office and that it's not in her Penguin or her Ladybird children's grammar either. She was, of course, an English teacher in her day. Her explanation contradicts the one on the commercial website. And as I parse the sentence again, I am getting a mix of present participles and gerunds as complements to various parts of speech which are in fact parts of writing, not speech. So I draw back into my role as a poet, not that of a linguist, and think of what the move to the use of -ing in the titles in this volume reveals about the way in which practitioners accent actions needed for creating welcoming environments, how they tell of ambiguity or fluidity in specific contexts and media. These are telling, telling of the need for hospitality, for an attention to what linguistic welcome might mean.

Collaborating
Working
Listening
DJ - ing
Sharing
Teaching
Using
Creating
Performing
Assessing
Building
Crafting
Filmmaking
Celebrating
Connecting.

2 The Well in Welcome

The chapters and examples in this volume have all responded to questions asked of participants about their educational or artistic practice for a project, funded by the Arts and Humanities Research Council, 'Creating Welcoming Environments in Schools'. The project is concerned with the fact that:

(1) Schools may not focus enough on children's own language resources but mainly on the curriculum and developing English.

(2) Schools rely on commercial resources celebrating other languages which don't necessarily cover children's own languages.
(3) Schools may not know which languages children know and use – the reporting requirement to (English/Welsh) government on 'first' language is known, but the richness in individuals and families is less known or patchy.

The problems with the examples given for the gerund are structurally the same as those outlined here. The focus on parts of speech and normative anglo-centric, westernised examples not children's own resources; the commercial packaging of the language by for-profit websites and publishers, however educational in orientation; and the confusion, insecurity, lack of a firm footing when it comes to knowing what is what, or what to do – the one which led me to phone my mum. All of this is contrasted with the 'richness', to use a phrase developed in Frimberger's (2016) work of pupils' own backgrounds and the 'patchiness' of organised, bureaucratised system knowledge, which is often focused on deficit models ('their lack of English') and not models of plenty ('there are four other languages spoken in the home').

A project with the positive title 'creating welcoming environments' is predicated on an underlying premise that environments as they presently exist are by and large not 'welcoming' and that attention needs to be paid to welcome, as a task. It's no surprise that in an entirely performance-driven system, where teachers, learners and carers complain of a suffocating pressure induced by a variety of performative measures, designed to fit out (school and universities) as places of 'therapeutic, technocratic, consumer militarism' (Brueggemann, 2007) that attention to such fundamental detail might be lost. At the same time, a system which is so stressed, in so many ways, which is given the task of creating welcoming environments for pupils have been through potentially traumatic experiences, needs to be in robust health, to continue this metaphor, to be good at welcome. Where schooling might have been repeatedly interrupted for newly arriving pupils, where long periods of no formal education might be recorded, and where systems of education have differed markedly, it is important that there is indeed a sense of education and the school as a sanctuary, not as a place where sanctuary has been destroyed (Farragher & Bloom, 2011).

The psychotherapist Sandra Bloom has worked over the years to identify the reasons for the crisis in mental health and community care delivery in the United States. Her work has identified systemic, structural fault lines which mean the system of care is in permanent crisis and hyper-aroused. Her words, introducing her Sanctuary Model, can be read across to many public sector contexts in the western world of 'service delivery', and they underlie the rationale for this particular project:

> Under these circumstances, the organization becomes unsafe for everyone in it. Emotional intelligence decreases and organizational emotions, including anger, fear, and loss, are poorly managed or denied.
>
> The crisis-driven nature of the hyper-aroused system interferes with organizational learning. When the organization stops learning it becomes increasingly helpless in the face of what appear to be overwhelming and hopelessly incurable problems. (Sandra Bloom: The Sanctuary Model (Bloom))

Hyper-arousal, hyper-vigilance, fear of missing targets, prescribed models of teaching, struggles to fit pupils with supercomplex, superdiverse backgrounds when compared with given, codified norms all produced repeated low-grade traumas of their own. A public education system whose employees are suffering stress and burn out is a poor environment for creating welcome, especially for those most in need of stability and structure, and sanctuary. What is interesting here is the need for the calm that will allow hyperactivity to slow and stop being overwhelmed so that learning can occur for all. A barrier to creating welcoming learning environments becomes that of the quick fix, the instant resource, rather than the re-sourcing that is time to learn something new, or a different way. And this is true, for our purposes of welcoming pupils seeking sanctuary, for teachers and learners alike.

The question before us – How can we create welcoming environments in schools? – becomes a question not dissimilar to the one I have worked on with my colleague at the Islamic University of Gaza for more than 10 years (Fassetta *et al.*, 2020). It is not so much the generality of the questions: How can we create welcoming environments in schools so much as the specificity of the common practical task: How can we create welcoming environments from which we can learn to live under siege; From which to be mutually restored? From living in hyper-aroused bodies to making welcoming, sanctuaries of learning require transition activities. Some of these need professional therapeutic or medical care, others need care, others need management, and others, learning. All need a language or a media in which the transitions can be expressed and understood, perhaps not cognitively, but certainly through embodiment. I do not wish to suggest here that those in the Gaza Strip, or those arriving from war zones, conflict and forms of enduring fear and oppression should have their experiences and suffering 'down-graded' to compare with those working in peace-time, performance-driven management systems in the public sector. What interests me is the way sanctuaries of learning which are welcoming can be produced structurally and systemically out of specific contexts which are already crisis-driven in their own regards.

3 Transition Ceremonies of Welcome and Arrival

I want to offer three transitions here that I believe are necessary. I emphasise transition activities here as I want to resist the 'pivot'; the quick, easy, well-oiled, technological and instrumental metaphor which suggests that at the flick of a switch we can move from a trauma-driven context of learning to a trauma-informed approach, from a specifying of education under an ideology of efficiency and performativity to one of creativity and welcome, before you can say 'Jack Robinson'. And there we have it again, a part of speech, so anglo-centric that the idiom will fail to do any welcoming work for Mariam Derwit or Mohammad Asif or Hope Precious Mutumbe. Transitioning is an act of translation. Translation slows things down, and, as I posited above, slowing things down from hyper-aroused to, let's say, curious, attentive, patiently ready means optimal conditions for welcoming and for meeting something new, different, strange, something to be learned.

The first transition takes place in ceremony, in schools. It is marked in this volume by the emphasis on celebrating, sharing, connecting, listening.

In Aotearoa New Zealand, and in many cultures worldwide, the work of welcome is ceremonial work, not a role call and a registration or pupil number. In a Pōwhiri, it involves clear protocols – who calls people in, who leads the newcomers, a call and response in song, not spoken words. Song, after all, is easier in a language not your own, than speech. It involves words spoken by elders and those entrusted with knowledge, wisdom and art. It involves dance, song and a visceral encounter with fear in the form of the traditional 'Haka'. In short, those things which get in the way of learning, of encounter, of good, peaceful living, are slowed down, ritualised and named or enacted. And once it's done, and the tight lines between the two groups have been seen for what they are, the lines blur and food and drink and art and also common prayer make up a new group.

This ceremonial dimension of transitioning to welcoming environments is extraneous to performance-driven managerialism. It is literally a 'waste of time' as anthropologists have described (Malinowski, 1922; Turner, 1995) and yet provides important social dramas and markers of the values of a community. In other words, if a welcoming environment is important to schools, then it cannot be done on the cheap or on the fly. The lean, mean performance-driven systems will not be sufficient. It needs to be lavish; it needs to place its markers of collective beauty in the space. It needs to be more than a charter on the wall or an off the shelf sign in generic languages that says 'welcome'. Pupils, parents and teachers all need to know it is meant, and meant well.

4 Welcoming Exiled Speech

The second transition is at the level of discourse. School leaders and practitioners all need to allow time and space to change the language and the languages. Time need to be taken to find out which languages are in a school and which are joining a school and how to make these a part of the specificity and distinctiveness of the environment. It's very easy for tokenism to be the default under efficiency and performative structures. For there to be a transition to trauma-informed structures and systems, there needs also to be a transition into new speech. This is work for exiles, as I've stated previously, are well-prepared (Phipps, 2010). Brueggemann (1997) insists that certain things characterise the practices of exiles – that we/they are careful about being cosy with Empire; that we/they are careful with the Empire's language [of managerialist ideology and performativity in our context, I would suggest]; that we/they tackle the dominant, failing script with words of our/their own. In this regard, this element of transition will be 'learner-centred' to use the present language of empire, it will be the speech of those who have fled, who have seen, who have arrived and who are saying things which are specific, and peculiar; words like 'my alarm went off, but I wasn't finished with my sleep' redolent with meaning, with poetry even, but incorrect, but the Empire's standards.

> To survive linguistically and emotionally the contradictions of everyday life, multilingual subjects draw on the formal semiotic and aesthetic resources afforded by

various symbolic systems to reframe these contradictions and create alternative worlds of their own. (Kramsch, 2009: 29)

I cannot prescribe this speech as it will be improvised from the experiences and language-scapes and practices of a specific school, 'Inhabitants the world over grow into the knowledge of how to carry on their lives by trying things out, often guided by more experienced companions, in the anticipation of what the outcomes might be' (Ingold, 2011: 15). It is improvisational work, and neologisms will come and enrichment of language as a result. What I do know is that this is the opposite of 'brainstorming' or 'creativity' as an assessment criterion. For education to be creative, the concept of 'creativity' will need a rest, a stint in the attic. The creative potential of neoliberal 'creativity' is exhausted. As Eagleton (2003) declared, 'The style of thinking known as postmodernism is approaching its end'. Jazz didn't come from nowhere under a command 'to pivot', 'to be creative' but out of a melting and blurring and meeting of sounds, old and new and experimental. New thinking comes from new specificities; 'It needs to chance its arm, break out of a rather stifling orthodoxy [race, gender, class] and explore new topics [language, arts], not least those of which it has so far been unreasonably shy' (Eagleton, 2003: 222).

In this volume, the language of this transition is represented by working, using, building and sharing.

5 Crafting, Making, Finding the Poetry

The third transition follows the work of Boaventura de Sousa Santos (Mehrotra & Mehrotra, 2016; Santos, 2014, 2018) and my own work on decolonising multilingualism (Phipps, 2019), together with that of Ingold's work on crafting (Ingold, 2013) and Sarah Cox's work with translanguaging and language ecologies with refugee families (Cox, 2021).

In 'The End of the Cognitive Empire: The coming of age of epistemologies of the south', Santos (2018) maintains that the dominance of critical thinking and educational systems in the westernised academy, and thereby also in the educational systems of the west, have failed. Their failure lies not in their ability to produce inequality, suffering, oppression and mass accumulations of wealth, but rather in their ability to end those inequalities, that suffering, the oppression and the grinding hardship of poverty. He lays the blame firmly at the door of the epistemologies of the north, the systems of thinking from the Enlightenment onwards which have privileged cognitive knowledge over other forms. Again, here, we are to be led otherwise, by those who are new arrivals, formed in contexts where knowledge is oralising rather textualising, where knowledge is carried as much in a dance or a cloth, a pause in the music, a proverb, a song (Sitholé, 2020a, 2020b, 2020c, 2020d; Tordzro, 2020a, 2020b, 2020c, 2020d).

In my own work on decolonising multilingualism, I've argued in that the work we do in future, if it is to decolonise, and therefore, beyond this, to be sanctuary, to be trauma-informed, to have balance, poise, and to be hospitable, it will need to be an art, and it will need to improvise, with a spirit of ceremony and of mischief.

Welcoming environments are those that are wide enough to be as safe as possible with the extremes of life and death, of trauma and joy, as well as the performance-orientated ranges in the centre. Traditionally in societies across the world, including our own, these are spaces held by artists, poets and by elders of spiritual and expressive depth. People who have seen a lot, thought a lot, held a lot and who know a lot but use spaces between words, silences, blank spaces and poetry (Phipps & Sitholé, 2018).

Poetry is my own preferred artistic medium, alongside drama, but I will gladly range. And schools where this is scope to range make for wonderous places of improvisation and expression, of ceremony and colour and making. When I make, or craft, or write, or play, I do so by fumbling my way across patterns, and designs laid down before, and then riffing off those patterns into my own felt expression. This is not some gift, or genie. It is practice. In his chapter 'Knowing from the inside', the anthropologist Tim Ingold (2013: 1) says 'It is, in short, by watching, listening and feeling – by paying attention to what the world has to tell us – that we learn'.

> Surely the most anti-academic of academic disciplines, anthropology could not be sustained were it not for the institutions of learning and scholarship in which most of its practitioners spend the greater part of their working lives. Yet at the same time, it is largely devoted to challenging the principal epistemological claim upon which the legitimacy of these institutions is founded, and that continues to underwrite their operations. (Ingold, 2013: 2)

It is from within the academy that Sarah Cox (Cox, 2020) has conducted her work with newly arrived refugee families and with the British Red Cross. In her work, she has taken a mutual language learning and translanguaging (Canagarajah, 2013) approach by beginning her language classes on arrival, not with the teaching of English words, but the learning of words from her linguistically diverse families. Here, she has challenged the principal medium of the epistemological claim legitimising not just the academy, but the process of integration and the linguistic dominance of English within the UK education system. She has not done this by arguing theoretically for this stance. She has not done this by collecting data on how much of language teaching is in one dominant language, and that of the teacher. Instead she has found a way of watching, listening and feeling – paying attention – so that she could learn from the families, first.

Elsewhere we have argued that 'English last' is useful principle in this work of making – as – decolonising (Phipps, 2019). This is about a reorientation of our dominant modes of working and knowing, like switching to using your non-dominant hand for tasks. It's awkward, but it's balancing. We are not saying 'no English', just asking for certain moments, or a certain art of learning, that English might wait for a while, until others have had their time in a medium of their own comfort, preference, even language sanctuary. This also goes for artistic work. For some, such work is intensely numeric, for others it's music, or colour, craft movement or spoken word. What we 'feel' in Ingold's sense above is often the intensification that marks a transition, a dance as a felt walk is one where we know we have moved our bodies from a place of habit into a different, less habitual action. The less habitual is the space of transition, the liminal zone (Turner, 1995). It is where social life takes account of its specific experiences, accounts for them, feels their heights and depths, and makes new steps. It is what is needed for welcome to be created well.

This transition is presented in this volume through Dj-ing, crafting, creating, listening, filmmaking and poetry.

6 The Well

The Well in Welcoming is the title of this chapter. It began in a hesitation around the knowledge base of epistemologies of the north. Is it a gerund or a present participle? Or both. Or neither? Running like a underground stream in the words 'welcome' and 'welcoming' is wel; well from which we have our word of the moment, 'wellbeing' or 'wellness'. It is also the word for a source of water, dug into the ground, to ensure life and plenty. The Well is a constant metaphor for education, learning and knowledge.

'Wel' is an old Germanic word. It is an immigrant word in our language; in fact, it is a colonial word, a settler, invader even. So is 'come'. But transitions happen across words too, and they can change and come wonderous offerings to our imagination. Those who enable such transition are the poets – 'meddling', as my friend and colleague, and poet Kofi Anyidoho would say 'in other people's business'. In 'The Place We Call Home', Anyidoho describes something of the improvisational origins of his poetry, and the echoes and soundscapes which fertilise them. With it comes a sense of the wellness of the poet, in paying homage, in a slower pace of life, and over the years, or wondering and asking where next? And of learning from beyond the habitual.

> In the end, however, regardless of when or where or how they originated, there was always a persistent elusive echo that rose and faded across the soundscape, fertilizing these poems into an endless yearning to pay homage to ancestral time and seek guidance into a future beyond the mirages of our daily human existence. (Anyidoho, 2011)

Mirages are not wells.

Following the mirages of performance management and the language of empire, we will arrive in the land that is not. Hostile. Deathly. No watering holes. Following water, as source, the well, an element not for our habitual living, but with lessons for us nonetheless, this double metaphor, of welcome and well come, might be a source for our transitions.

> *Poetic life depends on water*
> *Its ebb and flow*
> *Its life sustaining, giving qualities*
> *A Pedagogy for Oases*
> *A Pedagogy of Water*
> *The Well in Well Come*

Lamenting Aridity
Bureaucratic control
Urgency of Email
Forms in place of Form
Diarized Days
Assessments
Reviews
End of Trust
Ugliness
Lamenting Well
Thinking Well
Remembering Well
Being Well
Well-coming
The commonweal.
The source of wealth.

Remember to flow
Refresh
Rest
Drink

As metaphor
As material
As movement
Flows,
Ripples,
Pools
Rapids,
Shallows,

Ride the rapids
Be greeted by strange elements
Gasp at the drift
When the water is our teacher

Notes

(1) I am grateful for the increased confusion our call produced, and the ability to go to the source of my mother tongue, when the textual sources failed.
(2) I am indebted to Rima Andmariam for this linguistic and cultural example.

References

Anyidoho, K. (2011) *The Place We Call Home*. Banbury: Ayebia Clarke Publishing.
Bloom, S.L. and Farragher, B. (2011) *Destroying Sanctuary: The Crisis in Human Service Delivery Systems*. Oxford: Oxford University Press.
Bloom, S.L. (2013) The Sanctuary Model. See http://www.sanctuaryweb.com/TheSanctuaryModel.aspx (accessed February 2022).

Brueggemann, W. (1997) *Cadences of Home: Preaching Among Exiles*. Westminster: John Knox Press.
Brueggemann, W. (2007) *Mandate to Difference: An Invitation to the Contemporary Church*. Louisville: Westminster John Knox.
Canagarajah, S. (2013) *Translingual Practice: Global Englishes and Cosmopolitan Relations*. London: Routledge.
Cox, S. (2021) How can we better support refugee families in Scotland through an ecological, multilingual approach to language learning? In G.S. Levine and D. Mallows (eds) *Language Learning of Migrants in Europe*. New York: Springer.
Eagleton, T. (2003) *After Theory*. London: Penguin.
Fassetta, G., Al-Masri, N. and Phipps, A. (2020) *Multilingual Online Academic Collaborations as Resistance: Crossing Impassable Borders*. Bristol: Multilingual Matters.
Frimberger, K. (2016) Enabling arts-based, multilingual learning spaces for young people with refugee backgrounds. *Pedagogy, Culture, Society* 24 (2), 285–299.
Ingold, T. (1996) General introduction. In T. Ingold (ed.) *Key Debates in Anthropology* (pp. 1–15). London and New York: Routledge.
Ingold, T. (2011) *Being Alive: Essays on Moving, Knowledge and Description* London: Routledge
Ingold, T. (2013) *Making: Anthropology, Archaeology, Art and Architecture*. London: Routledge.
Kramsch, C. (2009) *The Multilingual Subject*. Oxford: Oxford University Press.
Malinowski, B. (1922) *Argonauts of the Western Pacific: An Account of Native Enterprise and Adventure in the Archipeligoes of Melanesian New Guinea*. London: Routledge.
Mehrotra, S. and Mehrotra, S. (2016) Technical and vocational education in Asia: What can South Asia learn from East/South East Asia? *The Indian Journal of Labour Economics* 59 (4), 529–552.
Phipps, A. (2010) Drawing breath: Creative elements and their exile from higher education. *Arts and Humanities in Higher Education* 9 (1), 42–53.
Phipps, A. (2019) *Decolonising Multilingualism: Struggles to Decreate*. Bristol: Multilingual Matters.
Phipps, A. and Gonzalez, M. (2004) *Modern Languages: Learning and Teaching in an Intercultural Field*. London: Sage.
Phipps, A. and Sitholé, T. (2018) *The Warriors Who Do Not Fight*. Glasgow: Wild Goose Publications.
Phipps, A., Sitholé, T., Tordzro, G. and Tordzro, N.D. (2020) English last: Displaced publics and communicating multilingually as social act and art. In E. Scandrett (ed.) *Public Sociology As Educational Practice: Challenges, Dialogues and Counter-Publics*. Bristol: Bristol University Press.
Santos, B.d.S. (2014) *Epistemologies of the South: Justice Against Epistemicide*. London & New York: Routledge.
Santos, B.d.S. (2018) *The End of the Cognitive Empire: The Coming Age of Epistemologies of the South*. Durham & London: Duke University Press.
Sitholé, T. (2020a) Hekani pa ruwaré. MIDEQ. See https://www.mideq.org/en/blog/hekani-paruwaré/ MIDEQ (accessed February 2022).
Sitholé, T. (2020b) Mazwi e Nzendo: Midziyo. MIDEQ. See https://www.mideq.org/en/blog/mazwi-e-nzendo-midziyo-itemsobjects/ 2020 (accessed February 2022).
Sitholé, T. (2020c) Mazwi e Nzendo: Sezvazviri. MIDEQ. See https://www.mideq.org/en/blog/mazwi-e-nzendo-sezvazviri-literal/ 2020 (accessed February 2022).
Sitholé, T. (2020d) Mazwi e Nzendo: Zvirevo. MIDEQ. See https://www.mideq.org/en/blog/mazwi-e-nzendo-zvirevo-proverbial/ 2020 (accessed February 2022).
Tordzro, G. (2020a) Hamadzi, memory as silence: Memory in sound, silence and the compassion of music. MiDEQ. See https://www.mideq.org/en/blog/hamadzi-memory-silence-memory-sound-silence-and-compassion-music/ 2020 (accessed February 2022).
Tordzro, G. (2020b) Hamadzi, memory as silence: Memory, language learning and remembering a forgotten language. MIDEQ. See https://www.mideq.org/en/blog/hamadzi-memory-silence-memory-language-learning-and-remembering-forgotten-language/ 2020 (accessed February 2022).
Tordzro, G. (2020c) Ŋutefe Ʋɔdriba (Memory Dragon). MIDEQ. See https://www.mideq.org/en/blog/memory-dragon/ (accessed February 2022).

Tordzro, N.D. (2020d) Se anomaa entua obua da: 'The bird that does not fly does not eat'. MIDEQ. See https://www.mideq.org/en/blog/se-anomaa-entua-obua-da-bird-does-not-fly-does-not-eat/ 2020 (accessed February 2022).

Turner, V. (1995) *The Ritual Process: Structure and Anti-Structure*. New York: de Gruyter.

Website: https://www.ef.com/wwen/english-resources/english-grammar/gerund/ (accessed August 2020).

3 Working With Community Filmmaking in Multilingual and Intercultural Language Education

Maryam Almohammad

1 Introduction

In the 21st century, some language educators call for multilingual and intercultural language education, focusing attention on the social, affective and multimodal aspects of multilingual communication that conflict with monolingual approaches (Blackledge & Creese, 2010; Canagarajah, 1999, 2013; Phipps, 2013). This approach challenges monolingual language policies, which lead to viewing languages and cultures in terms of hierarchies with different values (Blommaert, 2010; Weber & Horner, 2012), and advocates the integration of learners' multilingual repertoires, and encourages the performance of multilingual identities engaging not only linguistic codes but also non-linguistic codes, materials, bodies and emotions.

In such contexts, filmmaking can represent material, multimodal and multiliterate 'identity texts' which reflect children's identities, languages and cultures. The creation of multilingual, material and multimodal aspects of communication in additional language contexts is captured by the concepts of 'identity texts' (Cummins & Early, 2011), 'sedimented identities' (Rowsell & Pahl, 2007) and 'multiliteracies' (Cope & Kalantzis, 2000, 2013).

As already explored in Chapter 1, Cummins and Early (2011) argue that 'identity texts' are texts composed using learners' multiliteracies, linguistic and non-linguistic signs belonging to varied cultures. The production of 'identity texts' is one component of a pedagogical approach that addresses all forms of marginalisation based on cultural, linguistic, religious, economic and social differences. The performance of 'identity texts' is a process in which learners discover, perform and imagine their identities and communities. 'The identity text then holds a mirror up to students in which their identities are reflected back in a positive light' (2011: 3).

Similarly, the process of filmmaking creates what Rowsell and Pahl (2007) call 'sedimentation of identities' where films become artefacts that 'reflects through its materiality, the previous identities of the maker' (2007: 388) and the imagination of possible realities. The concept of 'identity text' resembles the notion of 'sedimentation of identities in texts'; the history and multi-layered identity of the producers are reflected in these texts. The text maker selects from a wide range of material and multimodal resources available to them in a specific context, time and space. Working with filmmaking and drama together in multilingual environments flags the importance of the embodied dimensions of language usage demonstrated in multimodal and translingual practices (Canagarajah, 2013). Canagarajah (2013) defines translingual practice as follows:

> Communication involves diverse semiotic resources; language is only one semiotic resource among many, such as symbols, icons, and images. [...] Semiotic resources are embedded in a social and physical environment, aligning with contextual features such as participants, objects, the human body, and the setting for meaning (2013: 7).

Filmmaking involves the assemblage of multilingual, multimodal and digital literacies and challenges traditional notions of literacies and monolingual language ideology and includes a range of semiotic resources. These literacies, resources and modes of communication vary across cultures, languages and contexts and are captured by the concept of 'multiliteracies' (Cope & Kalantzis, 2000, 2013). Certain communities might value a specific mode of meaning-making over the other, and thus, users achieve their cultural purposes by drawing on a cultural mode of representation (e.g. visual). Multiliteracies describe 'the multiplicity of communication channel and media' and cultural and linguistic diversity. Children and young people bring to filmmaking modes of communication and representation, which reflect their identities and semiotic resources that have value in their community.

Engaging students in multilingual and translingual practices in language education through ready-made films and audiovisual media is addressed in the teaching of English as a foreign language (e.g. Altman, 1989; Hill, 1999; Sherman, 2003; Stempleski & Tomalin, 2001), French as a foreign language (e.g. Vanderschelden, 2012, 2014) and Spanish as a foreign language (e.g. Herrero, 2018a, 2018b). The Manchester Metropolitan University language education team worked for more than two decades on research led-teaching using films, showcasing current good practices and arranging a European language conference on the topic. Contributors' case studies from the UK and Europe can be found in Herrero and Vanderschelden (2019). The pedagogic usage of films in these studies aims to raise learners' cultural awareness and develops their intercultural and linguistic competence while using new digital technologies available to learners. Herrero and Vanderschelden (2019) present a collection of international language educators who created pedagogical approaches which integrate new technology, multimodality, multilingualism and interculturality into foreign language classes (e.g. Dubrac, 2019; Seeger, 2019; Tomlinson, 2019).

However, this chapter distinguishes between the employment of ready-made films and videos and filmmaking in foreign, second or additional language contexts because the language learners take part in what could be called 'community filmmaking'. In this context, learners participate in filmmaking to create content about the school community or communities beyond. So what is community filmmaking? In the AHRC project Community Filmmaking and Cultural Diversity, Malik *et al.*

(2017) investigate the relationship between filmmaking and cultural diversity in the UK. The primary purpose of the research is to examine how adult community filmmakers themselves experience community filmmaking and cultural diversity and how this supports cultural diversity in the filming industry today. Malik *et al.* (2017) explain that 'community filmmaking' is an umbrella concept that can be produced in different ways. The authors define 'participatory community filmmaking' as the process in which the community entirely produces filmmaking. Social, economic and political perspectives, rather than linguistic, have shaped scholarship in 'community filmmaking', mainly in Cultural and Media Studies. However, there is a need to investigate the use of community filmmaking in intercultural language education contexts in which learners can be involved with peers, teachers, artists or community members in the production process.

Thus, the two main research projects discussed below on community filmmaking in language education have drawn on various theoretical perspectives: critical pedagogic approaches, identity and interculturality, multilingualism, multiliteracies and performative and art-based approaches.

The rest of this chapter will summarise two fascinating projects that used filmmaking with students working with different languages, semiotic and non-semiotic resources, materials, art, drawing, storying and technology. As mentioned earlier, there is a considerable body of research on using ready-made films in language teaching and learning; however, few research studies use filmmaking in teaching, learning and researching languages, cultures and communities. The following two projects can provide teachers with other ways of using community filmmaking, drama and technology with children and young people. The studies are based in the English language context, but filmmaking and the pedagogic objectives are transferable to any multilingual learning context.

2 Creating Filming With Children and Young People

Co-produced projects and collaborative research, where artists, young people and children, educators, researchers and practitioners come together, have increased in the past 10 years, due to AHRC Connected Communities funding (Escott & Pahl, 2017; Facer & Enright, 2016; Facer & Pahl, 2017), the Translating Cultures Theme (Frimberger *et al.*, 2018), Community Filmmaking and Cultural Diversity (Malik *et al.*, 2017) and Critical Connections: Multilingual Digital Storytelling (2012–ongoing) project (Anderson *et al.*, 2014) funded by the Paul Hamlyn Foundation.

Community filming and collaborative digital technology are examined by scholars in culture and communication, economic development, creative industries, social justice, creative citizenship, literacy studies, applied linguistics and multilingualism (Anderson *et al.*, 2014; Escott & Pahl, 2017; Frimberger, 2017; Malik *et al.*, 2017; Pahl & Pool, 2017). The purpose of the studies varies from the role of filmmaking in communities to address cultural diversity, politics, integration and multilingual education. 'Community filmmaking' enables the emergence of creativity in terms of both content and processes and in understanding people's identities, cultures, values, social practices and languages.

2.1 The 'Critical Connections: Multilingual Digital Storytelling' project

One of the major studies about employing filming in English as an Additional Language (EAL) and community languages is conducted by Anderson *et al.* (2014) in the Critical Connections: Multilingual Digital Storytelling Project funded by the Paul Hamlyn Foundation (2012–2014; 2015–2017; ongoing). The project emerged out of a community activism approach to digital storytelling and drew upon Lambert's (2013) firm belief in the power of telling one's own story as a critical principle in democracy. Anderson and Macleroy (2016) developed the process of digital storytelling to embrace children and young people's languages and cultures and stressed that 'When stories are created in different languages or combinations of languages, they often carry greater cultural authenticity' (2016: 1). Digital storytelling programmes connect schools with life outside and enable students and teachers to 'uncover and draw upon what often were untapped funds of knowledge in the home and community' (Anderson & Macleroy, 2016: 266).

2.2 Why multilingual filming?

Anderson and Obied/Macleroy (2011) started their work to understand the tension between monocultural and intercultural approaches towards language education in government policy in the UK. The project aims to enhance 21st-century literacy in schools using digital storytelling. Anderson *et al.* (2014) work with 'community-based' 'complementary', mainstream schools, Spoken Words poets (Hirsch & Macleroy, 2020) and the National Resource Centre for Supplementary Education and British Film Institute (BFI) to develop language learning and intercultural literacy as well as digital literacy. Primary and secondary teachers (50) lead project in cooperation with parents and 500 students (aged 6–8) from 16 schools in the UK, America, Algeria, Palestine, Taiwan, Luxembourg, Croatia and Canada. Making and sharing multilingual digital stories provided students with a richness that helped to develop plurilingual, intercultural and digital skills. The researchers adopt an integrated, critical and inclusive approach to language education by engaging with learners' mother tongue (e.g. Arabic, Croatian, Chinese, Mandarin, Spanish, German, French and Greek), EAL, and foreign and community languages. Multilingual filming constructed inclusive and intercultural space for learners, connected communities and schools:

> It challenges the view that growing up with more than one language in the home is a disadvantage and provides a space in which bilingual/multilingual skills are nurtured and celebrated and where bridges are built between learning in school and in out-of-school contexts. (Anderson *et al.*, 2015, Goldsmith University Blog)

As explained below, the research team trained learners and teachers to assemble a range of semiotic and material resources to create inclusive, multilingual and intercultural spaces.

2.3 How to create multilingual and multicultural digital storytelling films?

The project team defined multilingual digital storytelling films 'as a short multilingual story (3–5 minutes) made using photographs, moving images, artwork, sculpture, objects, shadow puppetry, stop motion animation, green screen, poetry, dance and drama' (Hirsch & Macleroy, 2020). These semiotic, visual and material resources are assembled to reflect on lived experiences, and the team emphasises process over product. Teachers and students produced the films under themes connected to community issues and negotiated every filming project's cognitive, linguistic, cultural and social demands. For example, students were asked to translate the theme of '*belonging*' using cameras to make short bilingual films in their community languages, foreign languages, English and EAL. Here is an example of the translation of the theme of Belonging through a Spoken Word Poetry Film: https://vimeo.com/219976715/. The researchers and teachers also created a *Handbook for Teachers* (https://goldsmithsmdst.com/handbook/), which includes lesson plans explaining the details of the process of some films' production.

The project places students' agency and voice at the centre of the learning process. Using languages of their choice, learners create their personal views and understanding of reality (Anderson & Macleroy, 2016). At the same time, teachers and students were trained and gained filmmaking skills that can be integrated across the curriculum. This helped in engaging learners on local and global issues beyond the border of the curriculum and develop active citizenship (Anderson & Macleroy, 2017). The research team celebrated the Multilingual Digital Storytelling Awards 2016 at the world-renowned film centre in central London. The work of schoolchildren from the UK, Algeria, Luxembourg, Palestine, Taiwan and the United States, among other countries, was celebrated with more than 20 films.

> It has been eye-opening to witness how imagining and creating stories, with others or individually, helped students to find pleasure in learning languages, to feel more confident about their own multiple linguistic and cultural identities and to share freely their experience laid open to the eyes and ears of a critical public. (Budach, in Anderson *et al.*, 2014: 6)

The films are made available on the project website (https://goldsmithsmdst.com/) to a worldwide audience, impacting the creative process (Anderson & Macleroy, 2016). In cooperation with the teachers, students initiate themes, planning, storyboarding, scriptwriting, translating, creating, reviewing, subtitling, editing and voice-over recording. Learners develop critical thinking by setting criteria of a 'good digital story', peer-reviewing each other work and as co-researchers exploring the project research questions (Anderson & Macleroy, 2017).

The themes include travel (e.g. A Tour to China, a Tour of Bohunt!, inside out, journeys, Haringey's Journey, Journeys of Ibn Battuta, Journeys of Captain James Cook, A Journey to Croatia: Did you know? and Journey Through My Music), belonging and fairness. The students selected the stories that provide personally and culturally relevant rich contexts for learning languages, including EAL. The films open the door for holistic learning, interdisciplinarity and connecting spaces (home, school, community and the world). As can be inferred from the titles, the stories take the children to explore their own and other worlds; they make them understand the familiar, make connections with the unknown (Anderson & Macleroy, 2016) or revisit the past. For example, acting stories of travellers, such as the Arabian and historical traveller Ibn Battuta, makes the children perform scenes of travelling around the world and using other languages. Children performed positive and effective Chinese and Arabic cultural and social practices when Ibn Battuta visited China. Body language and customs represent an aesthetic image of the Chinese culture in the imagination of the learners. Their choice of 'plurilingual repertoires' on the level of the individual (Ibin Battuta) and societies (Chines and Arabic) allows students to construct a translingual and intercultural experience which values Chinese culture (Anderson & Macleroy, 2016). The creation of digital stories enables the students to explore their own and world cultural heritage and challenge stereotypes. To represent the bilingual repertoires of the students and make the films more accessible, the students used a voice-over which was produced in the target language with subtitles in another language (Anderson & Macleroy, 2017). Using 'translanguaging' (García, 2009; García & Kleyn, 2016) can enhance learning, 'particularly where higher-level cognitive demands are involved such as in the generation and structuring of story ideas' (Anderson & Macleroy, 2017: 4).

Anderson and Macleroy (2017) employ digital storying, allowing learners to experiment with multimodal and multilingual symbolic systems: moving images, still photographs, artwork, dance, drama and music. In the meaning-making processes, learners critically engaged in the construction of their identities, cultures and personal narratives. Like Frimberger (2017), Anderson's and Macleroy's (2017) performative approach to digital storytelling draws upon learners' sensory experience and their connection to place. Defining sensory literacy as 'emplaced practice' foregrounds the role of place and its connection with the senses in human experience and learning (Mills, 2016, in Anderson & Macleroy, 2017):

> Literacy from this perspective is viewed as an embodied practice that needs movement and action: through digital storytelling, we investigated how students slowly learn to create real and imagined places that are meaningful to them and their audiences. (Anderson & Macleroy, 2017: 9)

The learners produced their digital stories with international audiences in mind. The stories in the film demonstrate how the learners move across borders from 'sites of learning' to their personal place, home and community forms of knowledge and questions of justice and equality. To make their voices 'convincing' and 'memorable', learners creatively engage in forms of art (drama, dancing, visual arts) and the filmmaking process which renders their work as a powerful intercultural, translingual and multimodal ensemble 'infused with an aesthetic sensibility' (Anderson & Macleroy, 2017: 12). The project focuses on themes of migration and belonging, which demonstrates learners' 'deep personal engagement with culture as well as an affirmation of student's voice facilitated through drama' (2017: 12). For example, two students from Greek origins at Broomfield School, a mainstream secondary school in London, collaborate with a Greek speaker teacher and a drama specialist of Greek Cypriot origin. They organised two drama workshops in English with the whole class. The workshops first introduced students to the theme of migration through short videos, followed by group activities, idea development, acting of short scenes, discussion and feedback. Having discussed formal reporting and reporting in the media, learners adopted a documentary style in their films. The two Greek students write their scripts in Greek and English. The learners introduced a factual question about migration ('Migration, what does it actually mean?'), question its reasons ('I wonder who is to blame. Is it my fault?'), criticise the lack of action ('Many leaders speak and promise for a better tomorrow, but who turns talks into actions?') and express hope in a lyrical form ('Just as the winter wears a grey cloak and then the distant hopeful spring with an optimism awaits') (Anderson & Macleroy, 2017: 12). In their film, the two students used green screen which allows them to create moving images in the background of 'harrowing scenes reflecting the migrant situation unfolding in the news media' (Anderson & Macleroy, 2017: 13).

Students at Europa School (a mainstream bilingual primary school in Oxfordshire) explore the theme of friendship and unfairness in a French-English bilingual film through the story of two girls – one French and one Syrian – who meet on a journey to France (see Figure 3.1). In this film, children investigate war and migration from a child's point of view and the feelings of uncertainty and empathy. Twenty-eight students, aged 10, selected the film's title, wrote the script using storyboarding and negotiated the presentation of their ideas using visual art and audio. The film shows the Syrian girl moving across borders from the desert in Syria to the harbour in France. Children draw people's faces, the sea and the ship on which the Syrian and French girls meet. The drawing and music reveal the connection between the two girls and a deep sense of empathy. The scene ends with the words: 'Tu pourras venir chez moi!' (subtitled 'Come play with me!'). The music, dance and play

Figure 3.1 Image credit: Screen shot of the French–English digital story Abandonnée (Anderson & Macleroy, 2017: 511)

captured through music were interrupted with pictures of a police car, Playmobil police figures, barriers and passport checks. The Syrian girl is in line with no passport hearing the French words: 'Vos papiers, s'il vous plaît!' (Your passport, please!).

'The narrative does not have an end – the audience is left with the words "to be continued" – an apt way for such young children to capture the ongoing situation of migration and stories of struggle and hardship' (Anderson & Macleroy, 2017: 18). In these creative intercultural and translingual narratives, learners negotiate their positioning and identities in the world as global citizens and the positions and identities of others.

> Through the agency allowed to learners in composing their bilingual digital stories, exclusionary barriers have been removed, borders of culture and curriculum have been crossed and a creative space for identity investment has been opened up. Seen through an artefactual literacy lens (Pahl & Rowsell, 2010), the digital works produced are texts which have arisen organically over time and in the process of which identities have become 'sedimented', illuminating the object of interest but also telling a story about those behind its creation and about the performance of multilingual selves. (2017: 21)

Learners exercise their agency through multiple voices, creation of meaning and resistance of monolingual and monocultural views of citizenships and 'the right to speak' (Darvin & Norton, 2014) for themselves and others.

3 Digital Storytelling During the COVID Pandemic

It is worth highlighting that the Critical Connections project is still ongoing (2012–ongoing). The latest 'Our Planet Festival' was an online event in June 2021 (see Figure 3.2) and included multilingual poetry, artwork and digital stories. The festival was held in collaboration with Deptford Cinema and included 16 schools, 20 films and 20 languages: https://goldsmithsmdst.com/digital-stories/. The children created stories addressing cultural, environmental and practices during the COVID pandemic, plastic, gas emissions and sustainable development. The children narrated their concerns over the climate, human and animal populations, thus developing the 'skills required for active global citizenship' (Anderson *et al.*, 2018: 205).

4 AHRC Connected Communities Project

4.1 Filmmaking on language, inequality and power

Escott and Pahl (2017) use drama and community filming to explore learners' understanding of how language practices are entangled with the material world outside. To uncover this relationship, some applied linguistics develop an interest in exploring the agency of objects (Escott & Pahl, 2017; Frimberger *et al.*, 2018) and materials, including the materiality of language. In this sense, knowing about language and literacy have been shifting to include languages, visuals, together with material objects (e.g. digital technology, social media, craft materials), gesture and non-verbal modes of communication (Escott & Pahl, 2017; Kress, 1997; Kuby *et al.*,

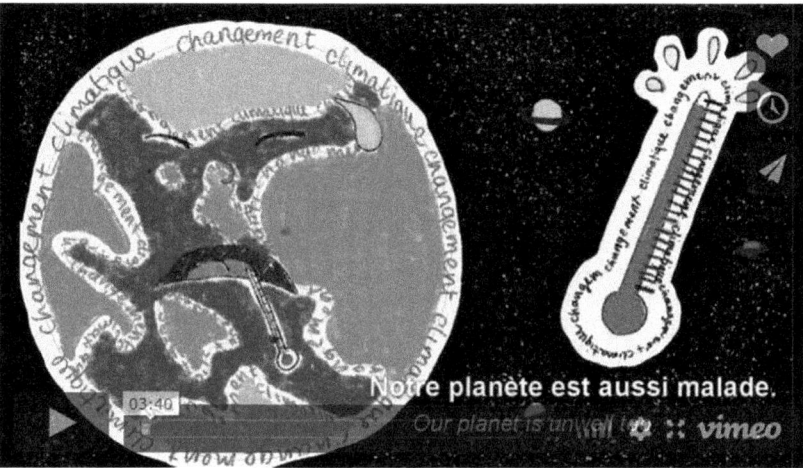

Figure 3.2 Image: Our Planet Festival filmmaking stories

2015). To help learners use their pluriliteracy skills, the research places children at the heart of the data collection process using digital media and children were taught how to make short films. The purpose of using digital media is also to engage children and young people in exploring the role of language in daily communication (Hall *et al.*, 2015). The authors are interested in how learners understand language in everyday environments and the role of language and other semiotic resources in constructing power. Thus, the purpose of the study is to address language inequality:

> As the way in which language is understood and valued dictates how individuals can successfully negotiate everyday interactions, everyday understandings of language have real authority and legitimacy (Escott & Paul, 2017: 4).

4.2 Imagineering and community filmmaking

Escott and Pahl (2017) examine young people's media production to understand how their language and literacy practices are entangled within objects and other non-human actors (digital technology, digital media, videos and films). The data for the project were collectively produced using digital technology. Escott and Pahl (2017) develop a lens for looking at films made by young people that acknowledge multiple modes and materiality within their meaning-making practices. They explored a pre-set research questions shaped by children's notions of language: What is language? What would it be like in a world without language?

Escott and Pahl (2017) asked young people to make films, write poetry, make talismans and tell stories. Five learners (10–11 years old) created the story below and the film when invited to respond to the idea of a world without language. The film was scripted and made in a playground context and came from a project called 'Language as Talisman' (funded through the AHRC's Connected Communities programme). The authors explored the use of everyday language in schools and youth contexts across Rotherham. The researchers created a collaborative space of practice within which teachers, young people, youth workers and artists all explore everyday understanding of language and the 'special nature (or not) of language' (Escott & Paul, 2017: 6). The researchers tried to understand young people's perceptions of the nature of language. 'Co-production' is located in collaboration among the researchers, artists, the children and teacher in the research processes and a focus on the film which answerers the research questions. The making of the Ninja was positioned in a discussion about 'the importance of language'. The film was imagined in a world where language was banned. Only people who had a 'paper permit' could talk.

Escott and Pahl (2017) initially explore the ways in which material objects were interacting with different modes within the boys' meaning-making. They then incorporated material objects into the frame of multimodal event. The authors described one incident where the boys demonstrated their understanding of language using a material object, the 'Talking Permit'. They placed language alongside visuals and gesture together with an additional column on materiality to make sense of a whirlwind of activity that centred on objects. The use of the 'Talking Permit', swords, ground and sound increase the young people engagement, the use of body language, eye movement and produce a sophisticated assemblage. Two versions of the story exist, one which narrates the Ninja from the point of view of human and one from the point of view of non-humans (see Figure 3.3).

This project is an example of community filmmaking that presents an alternative emagineering of language in society in order to uncover how language and material objects are complicit in the engineering of power relations. According to my interpretation of the Ninja film, engineering of alternative imaginaries about intercultural communication, speakers, experiences, languages, identities and powers are constructed around the theme of Ninjaness and role of the Ninja in society: The active citizens who claim their right to speak. The film, which was created through a process of co-production, is both an aesthetic and research object. Meaning-making is

Recount 1 – Ninja Story
"The film involves Ninja, Police Chief, Rookie, Newsreader and Cameraman (participants' names changed to acting roles) After the written credits presented to the viewer, over which the soundtrack involves a boy singing, in a deliberately high-pitched voice involving lengthening of sounds: 'It's a Niiinja stooory', the scene cuts to the playground. Newsreader explains that 'in a world where talking is banned, one Ninja will not rest until he has screamed his guts out'. Ninja comes into view and jumps around, swinging a metre ruler as if it is a sword and makes high pitched shouts, before hiding behind a bench. Newsreader announces that Police Chief and his new Rookie 'are going to investigate the Ninja'. They discover Ninja behind the bench and capture him. Ninja asks why he has been arrested. Police Chief explains that there is a law against talking. When questioned about this he displays his 'Talking Permit', a piece of paper pinned to his top, which says 'Talking Permit' on it. Ninja escapes and runs away. Newsreader is seen sitting on the bench reporting on Ninja's nearby noisy activity. Police Chief and Rookie chase Ninja as he does this. During the confusion the police notice that Newsreader is breaking the talking law and they arrest him. In the next scene, the police have lost both Ninja and Newsreader who then appear and stab them with their swords. At the end of the film each character was interviewed about why talking was important. In his interview Police Chief symbolically tears up his language permit asserting that 'I think talking is very important as well" Escott and Pahl, 2017, p. 7).

Figure 3.3 A Ninja story

informed by the children's everyday understandings of language, in-school and playground interaction, 'and an aesthetic informed by a shared cultural understanding of ninjaness' (Escott & Paul, 2017: 5). Escott and Pahl (2017) find the film 'an embodied understanding of the relationships between sound, language, writing, objects and humans'. Working with children made the data refuse to 'speak; instead, it sang, jumped, whooped, fell or was silent, resisting interpretation and instead, invited uncertainty' (2017: 6). Teachers can adapt the activity depending on what cultural values and material objects the students want to include and their stories.

5 Conclusion

The first project highlights global and local themes (refugees, the environment, belonging, journeys, cooking) in community filmmaking. The second project places filmmaking in community fiction, how children could imagine a world without language. Teachers could adapt this to other scenarios that can mix reality with fiction, and the themes can depend upon the pedagogical purpose and messages that the teacher wants children to consider (e.g. a world without harmful gasses; or the world post-COVID).

To conclude, community filmmaking is a tool that could allow students, teachers and parents to bring their languages, identities and cultures into the schools' borders to be celebrated, reflected upon and treasured by everybody. Filmmaking can also be used to engage students as global citizens and aid them in using a range of semiotic and intercultural resources. Finally, filmmaking can shift the focus to the learners' agency; learners can speak, use languages, perform, sing and write about what matters, and perform in a world where assembling semiotic resources to construct identity and stance-taking is power. Filmmaking creates welcoming spaces where all languages, bodies, ways of doing, being and cultures matter.

References

Ahmed, S. (2000) *Strange Encounters: Embodied Others in Post-coloniality*. London: Routledge.
Althman, R. (1989) *The Video Connection: Integrating Video into Language Teaching*. Boston, MA: Houghton Mifflin Company.
Anderson, J. and Macleroy, V. (eds) (2016) *Multilingual Digital Storytelling: Engaging Creatively and Critically with Literacy*. London: Routledge.
Anderson, J. and Macleroy, V. (2017) Connecting worlds: Interculturality, identity and multilingual digital stories in the making. *Language and Intercultural Communication* 17 (4), 494–517.
Anderson, J., Macleroy, V. and Chung, Y. (2014) *Critical Connections: Multilingual Digital Storytelling Project*. London: Goldsmiths, University of London.
Anderson, J. and Obied/Macleroy, V. (2011) Languages, literacies and learning: From monocultural to intercultural perspectives. *NALDIC Quarterly* 8 (3), 16–26.
Blackledge, A. and Creese, A. (2010) Translanguaging in the bilingual classroom: A pedagogy for learning and teaching? *The Modern Language Journal* 94 (1),103–115.
Blommaert, J. (2010) *The Sociolinguistics of Globalization*. Cambridge: Cambridge University Press.
Canagarajah, S. (1999) *Resisting Linguistic Imperialism in English Language Teaching*. Oxford: Oxford University Press.
Canagarajah, S. (2013) *Translingual Practice: Global Englishes and Cosmopolitan Relations*. New York, NY: Routledge.

Cope, B. and Kalantzis, M. (2000) *Multiliteracies: Literacy Learning and the Design of Social Futures*. London: Routledge.

Cope, B. and Kalantzis, M. (2013) "Multilteracies": New literacies, new learning. In M. Hawkins (ed.) *Framing Languages and Literacies* (pp. 105–135). London: Routledge.

Crutchfield, J. and Schewe, M. (2017) *Going Performative in Intercultural Education: International Contexts, Theoretical Perspectives and Models of Practice*. Bristol: Multilingual Matters.

Cummins, J. and Early, M. (eds) (2011) *Identity Texts: The Collaborative Creation of Power in Multilingual Schools*. Stoke-on-Trent: Trentham Books.

Darvin, R. and Norton, B. (2014) Transnational identity and migrant language learners: The promise of digital storytelling. *Education Matters* 2 (1), 55–66.

Dubrac, A-L. (2019) Playing the part: Media re-enactments as tools for learning second languages. In C. Herrero and I. Vanderschelden (eds) *Using Film and Media in the Language Classroom: Reflections on Research-led Teaching* (pp. 48–58). Bristol: Multilingual Matters.

Edge, J. (1992) *Co-operative Development*. Harlow: Longman.

Escott, H. and Pahl, K. (2017) Learning from Ninjas: Young people's films as a lens for an expanded view of literacy and language. *Discourse: Studies in the Cultural Politics of Education* 40 (6), 803–815.

Facer, K. and Enright, B. (2016) *Creating Living Knowledge. The Connected Communities Programme, Community University Relationships and the Participatory Turn in the Production of Knowledge*. Bristol: University of Bristol/AHRC Connected Communities.

Frimberger, K. (2016) Hearing-as-touch in a multilingual film interview: The interviewer's linguistic incompetence as aesthetic key moment. *International Multilingual Research Journal* 10 (2), 107–120.

Frimberger, K. (2017) The ethics of performative approaches in intercultural education. In J. Crutchfield and M. Schewe (eds) *Going Performative in Intercultural Education: International Contexts, Theoretical Perspectives and Models of Practice* (pp 21–40). Bristol: Multilingual Matters.

Frimberger, K., White, R. and Ma, L. (2018) 'If I didn't know you what would you want me to see?': Poetic mappings in neo-materialist research with young asylum seekers and refugees. *Applied Linguistics Review (De Gruyter)* 9 (2–3), 391–419.

García, O. (2009) *Bilingual Education in the 21st Century: A Global Perspective*. Malden, MA: Blackwell/Wiley.

García, O. and Kleyn, T. (2016) *Translanguaging with Multilingual Students*. New York, NY: Routledge.

Hall, M., Pahl, K. and Pool, S. (2015) Visual digital methodologies with children and young people. In E. Stirling and D. Yamada-Rice (eds) *Visual Methods with Children and Young People: Academics and Visual Industries in Dialogue* (pp. 186–193). Basingstoke: Palgrave Macmillan.

Herrero, C. (2018a) El cine en la clase de ELE. In M. Martínez-Atienza de Dios and A. Zamorano Aguilar (eds) *Iniciación a la metodología de la enseñanza de ELE* (vol. IV). pp. 65–85 Madrid: EnClaveELE.

Herrero, C. (2018b) Medios audiovisuales. In J. Muñoz-Basols, E. Gironzetti and M. Lacorte (eds) *The Routledge Handbook of Spanish Language Teaching: metodologías, contextos y recursos para la enseñanza del español L2* (pp. 565–582). London/New York: Routledge.

Herrero, C. and Vanderschelden, I. (eds) (2019) *Using Film and Media in the Language Classroom: Reflections on Research-led Teaching*. Bristol: Multilingual Matters.

Hill, B. (1999) *Video in Language Learning*. London: CILT.

Hirsch, S. and Macleroy, V. (2020) The art of belonging: Exploring the effects on the English classroom when poetry meets multilingual digital storytelling. *English in Education* 54 (1), 41–57.

John-Steiner, V. (2000) *Creative Collaboration*. New York: Oxford University Press.

Kramsch, C. (2009) *The Multilingual Subject*. Oxford: OUP.

Kress, G. (1997) *Before Writing: Rethinking the Paths to Literacy*. London: Routledge.

Kuby, C.R., Rucker, T.G. and Kirchhofer, J.M. (2015) 'Go be a writer': Intra-activity with materials, time and space in literacy learning. *Journal of Early Childhood Literacy* 15 (3), 394–419.

Lambert, J. (2013) *Digital Storytelling: Capturing Lives, Creating Community* (4th edn). New York, NY: Routledge.
Levine, G.S. and Phipps, A. (2012) *Critical and Intercultural Theory and Language Pedagogy*. Boston: Heinle Cengage Learning.
Malik, S., Chapain, C. and Comunian, R. (2017) *Community Filmmaking: Diversity, Practices*. London and New York: Routledge.
Pahl, K. and Pool, S. (2017) Community filmmaking. In M. Sarita, C. Chapain and R. Comunian (eds) *Community Filmmaking: Diversity, Practices and Places* (pp. 245–262). Abingdon: Routledge.
Pahl, K. and Rowsell, J. (2010) *Artifactual Literacies: Every Object Tells a Story*. New York: Teachers College Press.
Pavlenko, A. and Blackledge, A. (2004) *Negotiation of Identities in Multilingual Contexts*. Clevedon: Multilingual Matters.
Phipps, A. (2016) Educating the migratory imagination: A guide to the traveller. See https://researching-multilingually-at-borders.com/?page_id=1626 (accessed May 2020).
Phipps, A. (2013) Linguistic incompetence: Giving an account of researching multilingually. *International Journal of Applied Linguistics, Special Issue: Researching Multilingually* 23 (3), 329–341.
Phipps, A. (2014) *The Politics of the Body: Gender in a Neoliberal and Neoconservative Age*. Cambridge: Polity.
Phipps, A. and Gonzalez, M. (2004) *Modern Languages: Learning and Teaching in an Intercultural Field*. London: Sage.
Phipps, A. and Guilherme, M. (2004) *Critical Pedagogy: Political Approaches to Languages and Intercultural Communication*. Clevedon: Multilingual Matters.
Rowsell, J. and Pahl, K. (2007) Sedimented identities in texts: Instances of practice. *Reading Research Quarterly* 42 (3), 388–404.
Seeger, I. (2019) Addressing 'super-diversity' in the language classroom through multilingual films and peer-generated YouTube content. In C. Herrero and I. Vanderschelden (eds) *Using Film and Media in the Language Classroom*: *Reflections on Research-led Teaching* (pp. 30–47). Bristol: Multilingual Matters.
Sherman, J. (2003) *Using Authentic Video in the Language Classroom*. Cambridge: Cambridge University Press.
Stempleski, S. and Tomalin, B. (2001) *Film*. Oxford: Oxford University Press.
Tomlinson, B. (2019) Developing intercultural awareness through reflected experience of films and other visual media. In C. Herrero and I. Vanderschelden (eds) *Using Film and Media in the Language Classroom*: *Reflections on Research-led Teaching* (pp. 19–29). Bristol: Multilingual Matters.
Vanderschelden, I. (2012) Filmer l'école: un révélateur des identités langagières et des manifestations interculturelles dans la France d'aujourd'hui. In A. Lachkar (ed.) *Langues et médias en Méditerranée: Usages et réception* (pp. 227–234). Paris: L'Harmattan.
Vanderschelden, I. (2014) Promotion de l'interculturel par le film dans la classe de langue au 21e siècle: une approche multimodale. In A. Lachkar (ed.) *Langues cultures et médias en Méditerranée* (pp. 224–236). Paris: L'Harmattan.
Weber, J.K. and Horner, K. (2012) *Introducing Multilingualism: A Social Approach*. New York: Routledge.

3.1 Celebration Through Film

Gemma Sharland
Christchurch Church of England Primary School, Hanham, Bristol, UK

How do you welcome and celebrate pupils who speak another language in a school where the majority of pupils speak only English with fluency? This was the challenge that my school were recently faced with. After attending an inspiring English as an Additional Language (EAL) training day, I decided to solve the matter with a spark of creativity and maximum pupil participation. The outcome was a huge success and led to an inclusive project, which will be able to be recreated again and again as new pupils move through the school.

The school in which the project took place is a two-form entry primary with a very small percentage of children who have EAL. Four children with no prior experience of speaking English joined the school, and we were concerned that they may feel alienated amongst their peers, as the other pupils who spoke another language were proficient in English. We wanted them to feel welcomed and celebrated alongside our other multilingual pupils, as well as spreading awareness to our entire school population and giving a clear message to the whole school community that this is an inclusive school which welcomes all children.

With this in mind, we took the kind offer of Jane Andrews and Maryam Almohammad to collaborate with a local film student to create a movie with the rationale of celebrating the different languages spoken in our school. Because of our small population of pupils who this would apply to, this had to be a whole-school project including all ages from 4 to 11. We wanted the project to be child-led, so decided to gather all of the participants together to gain their ideas of what they wanted to do to showcase their talents. The end result saw several Year 5 and 6 pupils running the entire project – developing questions to interview their multilingual peers and interviewing them on film, scheduling the day, calling pupils out of class on time to ensure everything ran smoothly and organising any props needed. Meanwhile, our multilingual pupils decided on words or phrases they wanted to speak in their home language (e.g. their 'favourite' words) and how much of the film they wanted to appear in. The filming took around half a day in total, and we soon had a 'talking heads' film to showcase on our website, to parents and in a whole-school assembly. The style of the film was based on a Scottish Refugee Council film entitled 'Welcome to Scotland', available at https://www.youtube.com/watch?v=bl77CaxL_BA, created by Katja Frimberger and Simon Bishopp.

We were delighted with the result of the project and received great feedback from parents, staff and pupils. First, we were surprised at the number of pupils who knew another language, and many teachers expressed their shock in learning that someone in their class had, what had been, a hidden skill. Once we showed the film in assembly, it became clear that many of the pupils' friends hadn't realised these talents either and many of the film's participants were asked by their peers to teach them their language, resulting in several of our pupils starting up lunchtime language clubs. In addition, we then used the film when welcoming new pupils who have EAL. We had success showing it to both new parents and pupils who exclaimed excitedly when they heard their native language being spoken on the screen by a pupil in our school uniform – it offered a perfect way to show that we value them and their language and want to welcome them in to our school's family.

We also experienced a few surprising outcomes of the project, such as accessing special guest visitors for our celebration of Deaf Awareness Week following the realisation that one of our pupils knew British Sign Language. In addition, I was also given the opportunity to present a lecture around the project at the university to training teachers, encouraging new educators to consider creative means of engaging all pupils.

Our situation was relatively unique in that we had such a small population of pupils who were applicable for the project aims and that we were fortunate to be able to collaborate with a film student; however, I believe that it would be easily adaptable for other school contexts. For settings with a higher percentage of pupils who spoke another language, a single class, year group or Key Stage could create a similar film to then share with other classes. To extend the project further and into the wider community, families of the pupils could get involved, perhaps broadening the scope of the project to include learning about cultural or religious differences. Having an external visitor with professional film equipment raised the level of excitement and specialness for our pupils; however, a similar outcome could easily be achieved without film expertise with the use of simple technology and tools.

We were very happy with the result of our film project, and I am hopeful that the school will repeat and adapt it in the future to ensure that they always greet pupils who speak an additional language with a warm, welcoming learning environment which lets them know that they belong while honouring and respecting their home languages.

3.2 A Filmmaking Project

Alicja Lievaart
Elmfield School for Deaf Children, Bristol, UK

1 Introduction and Rationale

In the era of technology when even six-year-olds know how to use tablets, mobiles and apps, it is only natural that media has become an important component in children's learning. Elmfield is a small school for deaf children in Bristol, and many of our students struggle with learning English due to language deprivation in early childhood, late onset of language acquisition (both English and sign language) and cognitive challenges of processing language. Additionally, in the past few years, we have had more students coming to our school whose home language is not English, which created more of a challenge for teaching literacy. As deaf and EAL children have similar issues in acquiring English in all strands, including the use of a/an/the, tense consistency, pronunciation, vocabulary and comprehension, just to name a few, we have decided to develop a bespoke English curriculum based on the principles of teaching English as a second/additional language that follows what we know about the pathways of language acquisition for children.

Although many EAL students can successfully narrow the attainment gap in English and achieve as well as or better than non-EAL pupils (Department for Education, 2019), there are some who struggle. They will struggle to engage; they will not be excited; they may be 'cruising' through lessons nodding and pretending to understand. The same applies to deaf children. At Elmfield, engaging students and ensuring they feel valued and successful despite their being in the early stages of learning English is as important as English itself, so we were thinking how we could make our students learn language in an exciting way and give them the sense of ownership and achievement in the language that they so desperately needed. The answer was to set up a filmmaking project.

2 Planning, Delivery and Resources

The planning of the unit was quite easy and based on a topic 'Writing the World' from 'Skills for Writing. Units 3 and 4' by and Esther Menon and David Grant (2014). It covered a lot of non-fiction genres in all strands of English which is exactly what you want to teach effectively.

We started by watching a fragment of 'Blue Planet' on BBC iPlayer with subtitles on. The transcript was later provided to students, and they had to answer some comprehension questions about the programme. This was followed by a group discussion about the topic.

After that, we spent some time looking at and exploring DVD covers of different programmes about natural phenomena. This was aimed at learning about the features of DVD covers, both linguistic as well as presentation and layout. We considered the features of DVD covers where students had to label, describe and compare the effectiveness of each cover and the impact on the target audience. At this point, we asked each student to choose an area of interest from a different curriculum area (science or geography), find a 3-minute clip on YouTube about it and design an effective DVD cover for this clip including all the features had learnt previously.

At this point it is important to note that with this initial group, we used ready-made clips, so one could ask where the filmmaking is and whether it would be better for the students to do their own filming. This would be great to do, but our decision to use ready-made clips was a practical one as we had limited curriculum time to complete this work, and the actual filming, though undoubtedly a hugely creative exercise and great fun, would take the focus away from the language learning which was the focus of the unit.

Additionally, although they were not technically filming the source material, they did film each other while producing the voice-over, and they designed the DVD cover, researched and wrote the script, and had to edit the whole thing. As a result, they ended up with a new multilingual version of the clip. In the next cycle, with some other groups, we have used PowerPoint to collect images based on the topic chosen by the students, and we have added some animation effects and changed the presentation into a movie format and then continued with editing as we did with the ready-made clips. So, even though it could be said it was a re-creating activity, students were hugely excited that they had freedom to choose and control the content of the activity as opposed to a teacher telling them what to do.

Once the clip was chosen and ready, we then studied how to write a blurb and a tagline that would attract the audience. This included a lot of work on grammar, especially using prepositional phrases at the beginning of sentences and powerful verbs. After analysing examples of blurbs and taglines from DVD covers from the previous activity, the students had to research some facts about their selected topic (5 Wh-questions and 'how' was used to save time and guide them), consider the content of the chosen clip and write a tagline and a blurb for their DVD cover. At this stage, students had to use a wide range of language and literacy skills such as reading comprehension, critical thinking in order to select relevant information, expanding and securing vocabulary as well as writing effectively for a specific purpose and audience using correct grammar, register and topic vocabulary.

The next step was to start working on the voice-over and the transcript for the clips. Since the students had already done their research about the topic and the chosen clip, it was time to write a voice-over using the collected information. First, we looked at the voice-over from the first session. Students considered the language (including metaphors, alliteration, adjectives, powerful verbs, use of the present tense and plural subject, ellipsis, etc.), tone, pace, pitch to help them write their own transcripts and record voice-over for the clips. Students who use British Sign

Language (BSL) were asked to produce the transcript and translate it into BSL. We then recorded each student signing their translation next to the clip being played on the smartboard. In terms of our EAL deaf students who were oral and could use spoken English, they had to provide an English written version of the transcript, record the voice-over and repeat the same process in their home language and BSL.

At this point, it is worth stressing that this stage was extremely challenging and time-consuming, but it was definitely worth spending time and effort ensuring that students were able to work in English and their first or dominant language. Although English was still the target language and was the most important in the task, we wanted to celebrate and highlight children's overall language competency and use the theory of language interdependence and translanguaging (that is, effective code-switching between two languages and relying on one language system to support the other while learning new content or to fill in the gaps; see Park, 2013) to ensure maximum learning opportunities and retention of the target language. We strongly believe that this bilingual approach is very important for EAL and deaf students not only because of its impact on their language development but also because it strengthens their identity in both languages and makes them feel proud of who they are.

When it comes to the technical aspect, we used Movie Maker on iPads and computers to add subtitles, the voice-over and edit the clips. Some students used PowerPoint and images with captions and added animation to make it look like a film which was a positive option for some students.

At the end of the project, we used old DVD cases to insert the covers designed by the students (making sure that the design fitted the case!), and we burned their final clips on an actual DVD so that they could take their films home. We also organised an assembly to watch children's creations.

3 Conclusion

The filmmaking project turned out to be a great tool to excite and engage our Year 8 (ages 12–13 in England) students in learning English. Here are some outcomes that we have observed:

- high volume of receptive and productive language in English;
- successful application of a wide variety of linguistic and technical knowledge;
- engagement of higher-level thinking skills across all stages of the project;
- attainment above expected or at current performance;
- improved confidence and self-esteem;
- becoming resilient and overcoming the language barrier;
- developing a positive attitude towards English and learning of the English language not just the curriculum.

We will continue to use filmmaking with our students at Elmfield, and we hope that it will inspire our colleagues working with children developing EAL and sign language users. You can be as flexible as you want with this project: you can film it yourself, use any topic, any group size and any equipment. The possibilities are endless, and the rewards are great. So, let's get creating!

References

Department for Education (2019) *Attainment of Pupils with English as an Additional Language* [online]. London: Department for Education. See https://assets.publishing.service.gov.uk/government/uploads/system/uploads/attachment_data/file/908929/Attainment_of_EAL_pupils.pdf (accessed August 2021).

Menon, E. and Grant, D. (2014) *Skills for Writing Student Book Units 3 and 4* (1st edn). London: Pearson Education.

Park, M.S. (2013) Code-switching and translanguaging: Potential functions in multilingual classrooms. Teachers College, Columbia University Working Papers in TESOL & Applied Linguistics. *The Forum* [online] 13 (2), 50–52. See https://files.eric.ed.gov/fulltext/EJ1176970.pdf (accessed August 2021).

4 Creating Together – The Role of Creative Arts in an ESOL Classroom

Lyn Ma

1 Introduction and Context

The 16+ ESOL (English for Speakers of Other Languages) Programme is a unique programme for unaccompanied minors, who have arrived in Glasgow from many parts of the world. It has been running for more than 14 years and is currently the only programme of its kind in Scotland. In 2018, there were 140 Unaccompanied Asylum-Seeking Children (UASC) accommodated in Scotland under the age of 18 and a further 125 care leavers over 18.[1] In this chapter, I will outline the context of the 16+ ESOL programme, describe the overall approaches used and share how why creative arts are used in the programme (see Figure 4.1 for an example of a student's work).

It is not possible to access statistics on the number of UASC in Scotland at the time of writing; however, the Scottish Guardianship Service (run by Aberlour in partnership with Scottish Refugee Council) have had 165 new referrals in 2019 across 32 different local authorities. Glasgow remains the local authority with the largest number of supported young people, followed by Edinburgh. The vast majority of unaccompanied minors are from Vietnam (37%), Iran (12%) and Afghanistan (10%). There has been a marked rise in the number of unaccompanied Vietnamese young people seeking asylum in Scotland; of the 165 new referrals in 2019, roughly 100 were for Vietnamese young people. Precisely, 45% of unaccompanied young people have clear indicators of trafficking and exploitation.[2]

1.1 The 16+ ESOL programme

The 16+ programme is based at the Anniesland Campus of Glasgow Clyde College. It is part of the provision offered by the ESOL Department. The students on this course are young people between 16 and 19 years old who are either refugees or asylum seekers and are classed as care-experienced. In this academic year (2019–2020), we have more than 75 young people enrolled on the 16+ programme.

'Unaccompanied minors' is a legal term which means that students have often travelled, and now live in the UK, unaccompanied by parents or family members.

Figure 4.1 The work of students in the 16+ ESOL class of 2017–2018

They are often involved in the complicated and lengthy process of applying for refugee status in the UK. The programme is also open to refugees with parents in Glasgow, but these constitute a small minority of the programme's students. The programme was devised because the teenagers in adult classes struggled with both concentration on adult-themed work and with the social demands of fitting in with the adult majority in the class. It was correctly felt that they would do better in the company of their peers, studying on a bespoke and holistic programme – which is much broader than an adult ESOL one – that would address their needs as young people. The 16+ programme classes currently run at three levels: Beginners, Elementary and Pre-Intermediate levels, A1, A2 and A3 – Common European Framework (Scottish Curriculum Authority, SQA ESOL qualifications and the CEFR). This is where most of the young people are in terms of their language levels. There are, however, numbers of other young people students at Glasgow Clyde College who are at Literacies/A1 and Intermediate/B1 and Upper-Intermediate level/B2 (CEF).

1.2 Funding

The 16+ programme was initially funded via European money through the Atlas Project (http://www.atlasproject.eu/) between 2004 and 2006. Due to its success, from 2006 onwards, it became part of the ESOL college mainstream, funded in the same way as all other classes from Literacies to Advanced. The majority of my time as a senior lecturer is used to develop, coordinate and teach on the programme.

In 2018, it was confirmed that money from Glasgow Clyde's arms-length charitable foundation and the Paul Hamlyn Foundation (https://www.phf.org.uk/) would be used for a one-year project in which 16+ staff, including myself, would consolidate and develop resources which were shared with other local authorities and educational bodies at an international conference in June 2019. This project also funded independent research by the University of Stirling into the pedagogical approaches of the 16+ Course and mapped it against any other comparable courses.

HMIE (now Education Scotland) inspections have twice awarded our Programme Sector *Leading Innovative Practice* status, confirming its effectiveness as an example with the potential to be followed elsewhere. There is an article on our work online on the Improvement Hub of Education Scotland (2014) under Glasgow Clyde College: ESOL 16+ Programme.

1.3 Our students

More than 700 students have come through our programme, and increasing numbers of migrant teenagers are arriving in the UK in difficult circumstances and in need of educational stability. In terms of educational opportunities, one of the most important is the chance to study ESOL. Depending on the language level of the young person, some cannot access a school curriculum at Scottish Qualification Authority National 5 and Higher level/B2-C1 Common European Framework or study at National Qualification/National Certificate level, gaining a level of competency in English is a priority. The majority of young people arriving will have very low levels of English and may not be literate in their own languages. They will have had either no formal education or very fractured educational journeys. Therefore, before they can begin to think about future vocational studying or higher education, they need to gain not only confidence in English but also formal qualifications.

1.4 Rationale for the programme

As well as being able to access ESOL courses, this group of young people need to learn with their own peer-group. Not only is this pedagogically appropriate, it also gives the young people an opportunity to build social relationships and connections with each other. Given their level of vulnerability and needs, this group also benefits from extensive guidance and support as well as an age- and context-appropriate curriculum. In the past 14 years, we have created a curriculum that tries to address the specific needs of this group of young people.

The level of ongoing trauma that this group of young people might face is considerable. They may be dealing with multiple levels of grief and loss of family members, friends, culture and their future dreams. They will also be in precarious situations in terms of their uncertainty about their asylum status and/or the fate of family and friends in their own country. Some young people may have been victims of torture or witnessed torture and may be suffering from posttraumatic stress disorder, depression and anxiety. The need to be educated with members of their own peer-group who understand the complexities of their lives and experiences is therefore understandable.

1.5 Referral process

First, young people are directly referred to the college from major agencies that support them such as Glasgow Social Work Department, British Red Cross and Scottish Guardianship. Information is continually shared about the young person's well-being, attendance and progress. As the young person is seen by teaching staff more regularly than any other agencies, they are in a unique position to notice any changes in behaviour or any other concerns. Thus, the young person is supported in the most holistic way possible. This model is similar to that of a guidance teacher role in secondary schools.

1.6 Content of 16+ ESOL programme

The 16+ ESOL programme is unique in that it includes a variety of different curriculum subjects. These subjects are taught using topic-based lessons. There is a focus on using the creative arts, outdoor learning and participating in such programmes as the John Muir Conservation Award (https://www.johnmuirtrust.org/john-muir-award). This allows the young people to use English in a variety of non-academic settings and to use the talents they may have such as art or music. This helps young people's self-confidence and allows them to contribute to their own learning. In addition, teachers on this programme often create and adapt ESOL materials. This is because, traditionally, the majority of ESOL resources are aimed at either young English as a Foreign Language (EFL) learners such as European teenagers or adult second language learners and so are often not appropriate for this group of learners. Because of their lack of education or fractured education, many of these young people have not learnt independent study skills so there is also a focus in the programme on how best to learn.

Young people who have experienced and continue to experience trauma, loss and multiple levels of grief may have a lack of support network and initially may not have friends. We have recognised that they have a need to tell their story but can be unsure of who to trust. They may also have an inability to articulate their pain and distress, not only because of difficulties in expressing this through a language that is not their mother tongue but also having no experience or knowledge of counselling, therapy and Western medical and psychological interventions. Above all, they need stability, security and consistency in their everyday interactions with us as teachers as they try to rebuild their lives. It is with these factors in mind that we have developed our specific 16+ curriculum.

Over the course of the past 14 years, many of the young people who have completed the programme have progressed to postgraduate and undergraduate degrees, Higher National Certificate (HNC) and National Certificate (NC) courses.

2 Our Overall Approach

Our approach is in line with GIRFEC (Getting it right for every child (GIRFEC): GIRFEC principles and values) and SHINNARI (Safe, Healthy, Achieving, Nurtured, Active, Respected, Responsible and Included). Both are central to all Scottish government policies which support children and young people. This approach has been tested and developed across Scotland. The GIRFEC approach can be summarised as follows:

- **child-focused** – it ensures the child or young person – and their family – is at the centre of decision-making and the support available to them.
- **based on an understanding of the well-being of a child in their current situation** – it takes into consideration the wider influences on a child or young person and their developmental needs when thinking about their well-being so that the right support can be offered.
- **based on tackling needs early** – it aims to ensure needs are identified as early as possible to avoid bigger concerns or problems developing.
- **requires joined-up working** – it is about children, young people, parents and the services they need working together in a coordinated way to meet the specific needs and improve their well-being.

Although, as previously mentioned, our students have often endured traumatic events and journeys, we have found that they are also resilient, flexible and have incredible potential. For us, there are some key concepts that underpin our approach to building on this potential.

2.1 Working together

Our young people often require extensive support and guidance. Therefore, we offer one-to-one guidance and also work closely with all the other agencies involved in the young person's life. Our partnerships with Social Work departments, the Scottish Guardianship Service, accommodation providers and others ensure that we put the well-being of the young person at the centre of what we do. The young people know that we communicate with each other and can therefore respond quickly and appropriately to their needs. We do this by:

(1) All teachers on the 16+ ESOL programme have regular team meetings to discuss the progress of students and any issues they may be having.
(2) We are in regular contact with all the agencies that work with young people, including Social Work, Scottish Guardianship Service and other agencies.
(3) We ensure that the young people know that we communicate with each other and can therefore respond quickly and appropriately to their needs.

2.2 Belonging

Our specialist ESOL programme aims to offer separated young people a stable base, where they can begin to make connections with their peer-group and feel a sense of belonging. Having lost crucial attachments to friends and family as well as a sense of inclusion from their own countries, it is essential for us as teachers to try to re-establish connections and the sense of being not only familiar with a place but it belonging to you. We do this in a number of ways:

(1) We aim to create an atmosphere of safety and belonging – the class takes place in the same room each session and the young people are familiar with the space.
(2) Our classroom walls are full of work by the young people – this helps them feel a sense of ownership of the place as well take pride in what they have produced and achieved.
(3) We have pictures of places and things that might interest and uplift them such as maps, posters of beautiful places in the natural world and mottos and inspiring quotations from famous people.
(4) We try to limit the traditional 'talk and chalk' approach and use a task-based learning approach – this helps young people's concentration and allows us to break up tasks into more manageable chunks of learning. It also allows them to work in a pair or a group, and this helps young people make connections with each other and build relationships.

2.3 Building resilience

Our young people often face navigating the asylum process, learning a new language as well as dealing with loss of family, friends, their culture and future dreams. We respond to this by focusing on the personal strengths they already have such as courage, determination and flexibility in adapting to new situations to name only a few. By expanding our curriculum to include other curriculum areas, we encourage young people to discover for the first time or re-discover talents and skills they may have in Arts, Maths, History, Geography, Languages and other subjects. We aim to both challenge and support young people in building their sense of self-worth. Many young people find it difficult to recognise their personal qualities and abilities, and this is a very important part of ensuring they feel valued. In addition to this, many of the young people have had no education or severely disrupted educational journeys; therefore, we need to meet them where they are and provide learning experiences that help them remain engaged and successful. With some young people that means not making any assumptions and going back to the basics. They may need to 'learn how to learn'. We do this by:

(1) Offering opportunities to participate in a range of curriculum activities such as creative arts and team-building activities as well as maths and ESOL. We want to help young people to achieve their potential and to raise their self-esteem as well as understand their limitations.
(2) Including the John Muir Award (referred to above) as part of our curriculum because this encourages them to connect, enjoy and care for wild places. This is

hugely important for many of this group as they have come from rural backgrounds and have not grown up in cities. There is much research about the positive impact of being exposed to nature.
(3) Focus on providing materials that challenge and engage them. We create and adapt resources that are both culturally and age appropriate. This enables the young people to experience success and a sense of achievement.
(4) We do not underestimate the challenges they continue to face but believe that change is possible through the support of positive relationships with teachers and fellow students, through being given new opportunities and seeing things in new ways. We offer the Seasons for Growth programme, an internationally recognised peer-education programme (www.seasonsforgrowth.co.uk) dealing with grief and loss that comes from change. This programme offers a unique way to support young people to build resilience, make positive choices and be responsible for their own actions.

2.4 Being nurtured

We aim to ensure that young people feel cared for and respected. As previously mentioned, we understand that many of the young people will have a history of experiences that can be traumatic and that this can have a significant impact on their psychological and biological regulatory processes. We are not qualified to diagnose trauma, but as we usually see these young people more than any other professional working with them, we are in a unique position to notice when a young person is struggling. This can often be seen in their behaviour and demeanour in class; therefore, we are trauma responsive and work with other agencies to ensure our teachers are trained and supported to manage this. We do this by:

(1) Clearly explaining our expectations as teachers of the class and decide together what the rules of the class will be.
(2) Offering a flexible and caring approach towards young people who are struggling with anxiety, lack of sleep and are unable to be in class due to the many appointments they have with Home Office, lawyers and others.
(3) Understanding the impact of trauma, grief, separation and loss on the ongoing lived experience of this group of young people.
(4) Offering extensive guidance and building relationships where young people feel secure and able to trust us.
(5) Working closely with other agencies we support and encourage young people to access any other services that may be beneficial to them.
(6) Including important and relevant topics in our personal development strand of the curriculum such as sleep, staying healthy, making good relationships and dealing with difficulties.

2.5 The 16+ ESOL curriculum

Our curriculum has been developed by reviewing and refining materials we have created, adapted and used successfully over a number of years. It is designed to be used flexibly and can be differentiated for higher and lower levels of students but is focused on National Level 2 and 3 (Scottish Qualifications Authority) and A2/A3 (Common European Framework, CEF) levels. We have chosen six topics that we feel allow our students to explore key areas of a secondary school curriculum as well as develop their reading, writing, speaking and listening skills in English.

The six topics are bookended with My New Home as the first topic and Future Me as the final topic, and this can be delivered in one academic year. All of the topics are then divided into further subtopics such as My Country, Scotland and Glasgow, with activities that support the acquisition and development of the four skills. It also follows the design of traditional ESOL course books in that it teaches key grammatical structures and vocabulary at an appropriate time in the learners' journey. The resources also follow a chronological order. We focus on major celebrations and events when they happen in the calendar year, for example, our topic Heroes starts with resources about Martin Luther King and is designed to be delivered in January to coincide with MLK Day.

The inclusion of a personal development strand is a core part of our curriculum, so within each topic, there are activities that help young people identify their existing skills and talents and build resilience and connections with each other as a student group. Creative arts and outdoor learning activities are also embedded in the curriculum. Our resources are culturally and age-appropriate and aim to engage and stimulate our young people whilst offering a solid foundation for further study.

2.6 Challenges and barriers to learning

It would be disingenuous to suggest that all the young people we teach respond with enthusiasm to all we do and are successful learners. For many, the challenges they face are so considerable that learning is extremely difficult. In particular, many face the following circumstances:

(1) They have **no** parental/family supervision or support – this can mean that timekeeping and homework is often a struggle.
(2) Some young people have very challenging behaviour in class – this can be the result of many factors including mental ill-health, difficulty in sleeping, self-harm and trauma. Also, they may have never been to school and do not have experience of how to behave or study in a classroom. Students' fractured educational journeys can result in their view of learning being a very negative experience.
(3) Young people are living in a variety of settings including children's units and supported accommodation. There may be staff who offer support, but there may also be very demanding other children and young people living in the same place. Some young people are living in homeless hostels and bed and breakfast accommodation and for them finding a place to study at home can be a real challenge.

2.7 Why include creative arts?

Our curriculum was devised by teachers who wanted to find ways that make learning accessible and enjoyable for this group of young people. As part of that, we aimed to ensure that our classrooms were welcoming, colourful and stimulating places, where students' work was displayed and celebrated, a place where we could offer young people ways to celebrate all the stories, talents, skills and personal qualities of each young person. We needed to create classrooms with walls that mirror what is usually seen on the walls of primary and secondary school classrooms not FE colleges. In doing so, we found that we discovered a number of important things about our students.

(1) Many of them were very creative and talented. They enjoyed the opportunity to share and show these talents to each other and to us as teachers.
(2) The use of creative arts allowed a different type of learning and collaboration to take place. Often young people who were the least confident in the four skills (speaking, listening, writing and reading) taught in a traditional ESOL class were the most able and confident when it came to creative activities. Thus, they were able to use those skills and talents to help others in the class in a way that would not have been possible without the inclusion of art activities. This has a powerful effect on their self-confidence and sense of belonging to the class group.
(3) We found that by allowing young people control over what they shared creatively, giving space and time for them to explore their memories of both the joys and sufferings of their lives, both in their past and in their present, meant a unique and powerful understanding can grow between both the young people and us their teachers. Using creative activities allowed them to share, often without the need for language, their hopes, dreams and fears about their world now and in the future.
(4) Young people felt a sense of ownership, responsibility and belonging in the space that is their classroom.
(5) In allowing creative arts a space in class, young people told us they felt 'relaxed', 'happy' and 'had fun'.

2.8 Creative arts activities

Over the years that the programme has been running, we have tried many different types of creative activities, including filmmaking, photography, creative writing and visual art. I have chosen four activities that have proved to be most successful to the majority of students which are outlined below. All of these activities can be done with the minimum amount of equipment and resources. Our aim with both group and individual activities is to provide opportunity for self-expression that is not language dependent and allows connections and sustained relationships between students and teachers to flourish.

3 Murals

3.1 Our message to you

Before we began to make the class mural (see Figure 4.2), students worked in small groups to decide what words they felt were most important to send as a

Figure 4.2 An example of a mural made by 16+ students

message to staff and students at the college. They made a list of up to words and then as a whole class we decided on a final list we agreed on. The young people were also invited to write the words in their own languages.

We then used a large sheet of white material and used spray paint to colour it. The young people chose background colours of blue and white. When the sheet was dry, we then divided each section up and small groups of students wrote the words chosen in English and their own languages. We hung the mural in the corridor outside our classroom.

The young people were very pleased with the end result of this, and it was a very easy and adaptable activity.

4 Self-Portraits

This is a very simple activity that we normally do at the beginning of the academic year (see Figure 4.3). However, it can turn out to be very revealing. The young people were asked to draw a self-portrait, they can choose any aspect of themselves they wanted to draw, some choose to only do their eyes for example, some the whole body, but most chose to do the head. Some of the young people loved this, and the activity clearly showed their artistic talents; others struggled and said 'I can't draw teacher!' After reassurance that they didn't need to be realistic in any way and the main purpose was to have fun and try some students found it easier. I also encouraged students to help each other and so everyone managed to do something and the activity worked well.

52 Creating Welcoming Learning Environments

Figure 4.3 Self-portraits of 16+ ESOL students

5 Suitcases

5.1 What did I bring with me?

This is an activity best done at the beginning of the year. Instead of asking young people to write or tell stories of their family, friends and countries and thus risk causing emotional distress, making a suitcase that illustrates some of those precious memories allows for a visual sharing of cultures, and a place to share precious memories and hopes for the future (see Figure 4.4).

Before making a suitcase, the students are asked to think about what they have brought with them, not in any material sense as they have obviously left most things behind on the journey to the UK but in a more metaphorical way. Using a simple worksheet that asks the following questions as prompts, they can think of images and words to fill their suitcase with.

Examples of worksheet questions:

(1) *What colours do you see when you remember your country/city/village?*
(2) *What food do you remember?*
(3) *What objects do you think are important to you? For example, a Quran, a cross, a watch, etc.*
(4) *What do you think you brought with you? Memories of playing football in the village, swimming in the sea, etc.*

The students are then invited to share any of the answers with the whole class. Often, if students are from the same country, there will be shouts of recognition as ideas are shared. The next step is to collect images from magazines or the internet to cut and add to the decoration of the suitcase. They can also draw, add words or decorate the suitcase in any way they like. The suitcase itself can be made very simply with brown folders or a more substantial suitcase could be created from a cardboard box. The students can then share what is in their suitcase in small groups or as a whole class. The suitcases are then displayed in the classroom.

Figure 4.4 16+ ESOL student suitcases

6 Identity Boxes

6.1 Who am I and what do I want you to know about me?

Throughout this academic year, students have been exploring how they define their identity, what are the important and precious things they have brought with them from their own cultures and places of origin, and what they might dream of being and doing in the future. This is an activity that can be seen as an extension of the suitcase activity. It is in 3D and takes some time and so is probably best done towards the end of an academic year when the students are used to doing creative activities in the class. It can be linked to language skills such as reading and research, writing activities, as well as other relevant curriculum areas such as History, Geography and Personal, Social and Health Education (PSHE). The inspiration for the identity boxes comes from the work of Joseph Cornell, an American artist (https://www.josephcornellbox.com/) (see Figure 4.5).

They are made from shoe boxes that are then crafted by students over a number of weeks with resources and materials that are chosen and sometimes made by the students. The key concept of this activity is that the students are choosing how they want to represent themselves to others. They have complete freedom of what to include in their box and how they decorate it. It is not necessarily an accurate representation of them or their story, rather an opportunity to explore parts of who they are now and who they may wish to be in the future (see Figure 4.6).

After explaining the concept of an identity box and showing the students examples of boxes made by other students, they then begin to think about what they want to include in theirs.

Figure 4.5 Joseph Cornell, "**Homage to Juan Gris**" (1953–1954)

Figure 4.6 Some of the Identity Boxes made by 16+ students

Students are asked to make a list of all the skills, talents and qualities they have. This is building on work that has already been done through the year, encouraging young people to identify and discover all of the positive skills and personal qualities they have. These can include courage, reliability, flexibility, being a good friend, good at maths or can speak five languages.

Students are also asked to imagine themselves in five years' time and what would they like their lives to be like then. Questions to prompt discussion and thought can be related to where they will live, who they will live with and what they will be doing. This can be quite a challenge for some young people, so gentle encouragement is sometimes needed to help them see what might be possible. The young people then

56 Creating Welcoming Learning Environments

Figure 4.6 *Continued*

choose how to decorate their boxes, and their choices offer us a fascinating and moving insight into how they see themselves now and their future hopes and dreams and what they have chosen to share with the audience about their inner lives.

7 Conclusion

When words are not adequate enough and when the language you speak is not understood in the place you live in, creative arts can provide a way to express the deepest things within us. By using the creative arts to explore their stories, identities, hopes and dreams, our students can create very powerful and moving pieces of art. They can offer a way to express the many different parts of who we are and as teachers we may learn so much more about our students. For second language learners, they can experience the pleasure of exploring, creating, sharing and connecting with each other and us as their teachers.

Notes

(1) Social work with Unaccompanied Asylum-Seeking Children in Scotland.
(2) New Scots Core Group Meeting, 25 February 2020.

4.1 Working With Children's Needs and Preferences Using Creative Techniques

Su Tippett
Culverhill School, Yate, Bristol, UK

1 Background to the School

My work with young people is in a special school that provides a holistic education for 135 pupils (aged 7 to 16) who have complex learning difficulties. We offer an educational system that is based around children's neurodiversity, and it aims to create an environment that can be life-changing for the young person, their family and the wider community. Many of our young people are developing English as an Additional Language (EAL).

Sometimes it is difficult to understand how to access the young person's requirements and strengths. By looking at the student holistically, we are able to first, and most importantly, strip back the students' preconception of their learning experiences/barriers to learning so far, in their previous school environments. We can then access and promote the student, developing their resilience and their willingness to join in the learning process. The students' well-being is important to us, so whilst we are aware of the learning opportunities we provide (either 1 to 1 or whole class), we need at the same time to have high expectations of the student and their learning experiences have to be achievable and measurable.

2 Pedagogic Approach

In my opinion, 'Crafting' is a curious term to use in the world of education. However, in our school, we have found that art-based practices have helped students develop a sense of worth when teachers and class staff teams develop effective practice to support hard-to-reach students or students who may appear less engaged in their learning. A simple colouring sheet and a few pens/coloured pencils or chalks on the playground can create peer groups within a whole class environment. For students who are lucky enough to speak additional languages (EAL students) but may find it tricky to find the right word, crafting/educational focused design topics or projects are so diverse that we can create bespoke learning experiences for the staff and students.

We have found that by using a creative learning experience, we can find out about cultural backgrounds and communities. We can create expectations and discover gaps in learning and language, and by spending quality time with students on a regular basis, we have seen that students grow in confidence, with the knock-on effect being improved attainment. We have learned that students who have special educational needs or a disability as well as developing EAL often benefit from an interactive approach to their learning, such as practice in social conversation in a place where the student feels safe to make mistakes.

At an interpersonal level, we found that creative activities needed to include time for thinking/processing which supports students who are shy or lack confidence to talk to adults. As a teaching assistant, I felt it was a privilege to engage in conversation with students in 1-to-1 sessions, and this needs to be earned by the facilitator. It is a mistake to presume that students will want to work in this way – common ground needs to be established and a shared art or other creative experience could open up a conversation.

The location of the sessions was equally important for the student. The activity ideally should take place in the same environment and at the same time. Providing frequent positive reinforcement enables students to try activities independently or with support and gives them the confidence to accept that it's ok to make mistakes. Give time for explanations of language. SEND students with EAL find most, if not all, language technical and giving them time to process this will enhance their understanding and use. We celebrated successes with certificates and other appropriate means. However small you may think the success has been, it will probably be a big success to the student, and we think it is important to show and share work at the end of the project.

We support students with their faith circumstances – more confident students become ambassadors for their faiths. Mental well-being is vital. Connecting with people around you and trying something new helps with this, and as part of this process, we have used the Suitcase Project (inspired by the work of Lyn Ma, see Chapter 4). The students start off with the suitcase shape, but they may not know that it is a suitcase and the concept of going on holiday may not be the first thing they think of (especially if you have moved from one country to another and all you have is a suitcase/day bag/holiday bag). Accept that the student may not want or have the words they want to use so a translation app may come in handy or a dual language dictionary.

3 Details About the Suitcase Activity

To begin the activity, I asked the students to… 'Show me what you would like me to know about you!' No written words were required – just pictures and/or conversations. In most cases, this project took a term to complete, and at the end, students were given the chance to share their work with the Head Teacher, Deputy Head and special persons (normally a class team member). Students shared details about their lives such as special times, births, deaths, weddings, holidays and places of special spiritual significance. All students proudly shared their home language, and we were proud to listen.

For this project, the sessions were always 1 to 1 (me with an individual student) in the same room every week for 2 terms, the same time, the same place. Most sessions lasted approximately 20 to 30 minutes, and it was interesting that the students always wanted to stay longer. There were minimal interventions from me, as the facilitator, and students had the use of a computer for pictures or they could bring pictures from home or draw their ideas. One student continued to create their suitcase long after their session had finished.

Using the computer for pictures gave students time to talk about their selection and why they wanted to use the picture. Within the session, the students could choose music that they liked – so the sessions were student-led, with minimum interference from the facilitator. I just set the scene and was there to provide materials they may have needed.

Observations were taken while the student worked, and if the students mentioned anything, this would be noted and forwarded to the relevant school department and/or staff teams. These observations created a wealth of evidence that could support the students' learning and targets. Staff teams could then respond and if required ask me to work on certain aspects of the students' learning in later sessions.

In my opinion, one of the best discoveries was that during the 1-to-1 sessions the students would talk in their home language. As the student's confidence increased, they would share their work/language with the deputy head when the student felt ready, and, by sharing their suitcase, they could speak with confidence and would be open to questions on their terms. This may have been the only opportunity when the student felt comfortable to do this. I tried to overlap the session with the next student so that students were aware of each other within the school.

4 What Next?

To ensure the continuation of this project, it needs to be understood by the whole school that it takes time and that you must consider the student may have the right phrase in four different languages! Finding the one that is right for the occasion can be embarrassing, frustrating or annoying for the student. Language barriers exist, and we need to have a flexible approach to learning and teaching styles.

To maintain links with home and make school accessible to the whole family, we need to make sure families are welcome in school, and we need to be able to carefully explain and encourage a whole school approach about effective communication.

The school wants all the students to be confident young people, and we do not want students to use echolalia as a primary method of communication. The Suitcase Project gives access to breaking down this learned response, giving the child their own voice and the ability to show their work with confidence and creating confident communicators who can enjoy celebrating things that are important to them. They can share their uniqueness in a positive and holistic way and know they are being listened to and avoid feeling afraid.

In conclusion, the Suitcase Project has been successful on many levels. When facilitating this project, you need to consider everything, yet assume nothing as the activity is student-led and student-focused. You need to be willing to learn yourself, laugh with the student, use proactive listening techniques and praise and develop the student with subtlety and compassion. This project takes time as you are both learning and the student may reveal sensitive issues about themselves. Always report these, however insignificant you may think they are, as you may be the only person they talk to about these sensitive, personal issues. Do not change the language and keep your notes factual and exactly as the student said.

This project is accessible to all students, so if you have students with special educational needs and disabilities in your setting, this learning experience is a perfect example of an activity that can be differentiated in a whole class setting.

To help with school evaluations, we can say this is the way we meet the needs of the student, enabling them to feel part of the school family/community as well as improving their general well-being. The project has improved the students' self-image, and we have been able to incorporate their life skills development, which in turn develops resilience and independence. When the project has been incorporated into the curriculum, it has improved engagement, behaviour and confidence, and the impact of the EAL sessions has included increased interaction and communication skills. This means that the students we work with are understanding more, knowing more and remembering more.

My final reflection is that the suitcase itself is a wonderful window to the student, a good starting point to develop an understanding of the student (and the student of you, as an educator) the things that they know about, the things that are important to them. It also provides an opportunity for the student to be actively listened to, to have a small amount of time to look forward to/set a side in a week to express and be themselves creatively, to laugh and may be reflect on the week's ups and downs to be able to talk about situations in class maybe something they didn't understand. The session gave the students a place to ask for help without being embarrassed that they couldn't find the right word in class, plus the students teach the facilitator more about themselves which could be shared in the wider school community. The whole of the curriculum can be covered in the suitcase idea!

4.2 Assessing Children's Language Using Creative Techniques

Judith Prosser
Blaise High School, Bristol, UK

Inspired after returning from a workshop held at UWE on Using Creative Arts Methods in Language Classrooms, I immediately ordered a set of plain cardboard pizza boxes from Amazon, which were going to be transformed into 'Identity Suitcases' by my lovely group of Year 7 students (aged 11), who I had assessed to be around the early stages of English acquisition (see Figure 4.2.1 for some of the students' creations). Lyn Ma, who led the workshop, had originally undertaken this project with Post 16 students from refugee backgrounds with the aim of helping them deal with past trauma (more details in Lyn Ma's Chapter 4, this volume), but my intention was just to use this exercise to open conversations with the children. Each student makes a plan, gathers resources and then creates an identity suitcase. It is each student's own decision about what they choose to put into their suitcase and also what they choose to reveal about themselves (examples shown on the photos above); it helps to show both what is important to them and how they want others to see them.

My group of Year 7 students came from highly diverse backgrounds; some had refugee status, others were economic migrants and one was accompanying a parent studying for a PhD. All of these children had had to cope with great changes in their lives: settling in a new country, in a new school, separated from family and friends with only enough English to express their basic needs. I was keen for the students to benefit from the therapeutic value of this project, but I also wanted to exploit the opportunities for developing their English language skills. Before starting on the practical work, I created language scaffolds to facilitate giving explanations and instructions, describing processes and so on. However, in the end, the speaking and listening assessment opportunities were far richer than I had envisaged. After the students had completed the crafting stage of the process I talked with them about their suitcase and opened it up to wider issues of what they had offered, using these prompts:

- What would you like to tell us about your suitcase?
- What's the most exciting thing that has happened to you in your country?
- Do you have any stories you'd like to tell us?

Student A's home language was Punjabi, and he had been educated through the medium of Italian. He had great storytelling skills and was able to use vocal expression and physical gestures to communicate. This seemed to have an infectious effect

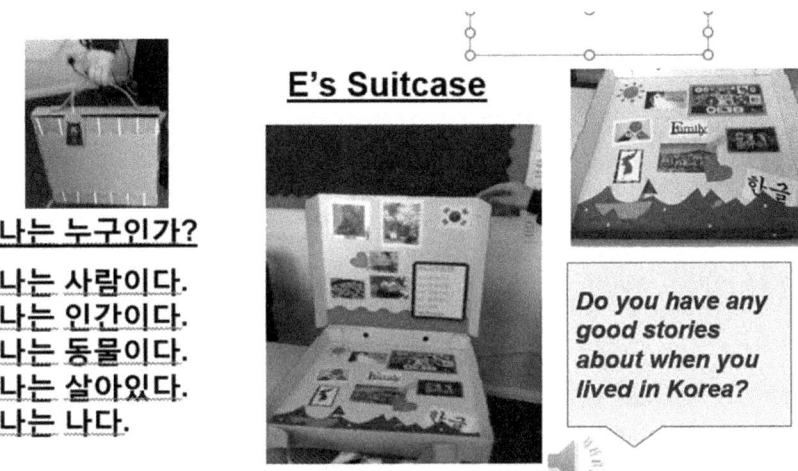

Figure 4.2.1 Crafting suitcases

on the other students, who began to compete with each other about who could tell a story that would gain the biggest reaction from their audience. The students had ownership of these stories because they knew them by heart and were drawing on their ability to translanguage; they were telling stories that had probably been told many times from different perspectives by different members of their family. The students were now motivated to use their computer tablets, or bilingual dictionaries, to choose just the right word or phrase for their audience. I decided for my own professional development that it would be beneficial to record the students telling their stories and make transcripts so that I could analyse the range of vocabulary and grammatical structures they used. Some students were reluctant to be recorded at first and some stories lost spontaneity, but they were all proud of their efforts, and many requested copies to share at home so that parents could listen to them telling their stories in English.

The three transcripts below provide evidence of speaking skills at the Early Acquisition stage of English proficiency and some elements of next level using the Bell Foundation Assessment Framework (see reference below). After completing this project, I realise that my previous practice of using so-called formal assessment activities, I had underestimated students' speaking skills. To my great delight, my students were now demonstrating the ability to confidently narrate in English, using a range of tenses with some grammatical errors and beginning to extend sentences with conjunctions.

1 The Thief, by Student A, 11 Years Old, L1 Punjabi

When I was-when I was 5 years old. I was in Italy and it was um 11 o'clock er in the-in the night. And I hear heavy footsteps and I just tell to my mum and she said it it's just your imagination. And I go in the living room and there was just the shade-ow of a person and I scream and he push me and he ran out. I was so scared and my mum said, 'I'm sorry I didn't trust you.'

2 The Young Train Driver, by Student B, 12 Years Old, L1 Hungarian

I drove a train home because it was late at night so the other train drivers couldn't see but everyone else in the train … So one of them left me inside one and I drove in in his lap-I drove the train. And that's when I became a big train fan. And I was so annoyed because my dad had driven bigger ones and I wanted to drove them as well.

3 Hot Pink Pants, by Student C, 13 Years Old, L1 Korean

When I was in -when I was young, I was in Koreas primary school, I wear -I weared hot pink coloured pants to school-long pants. And um, I thought it was perfect. And I went to school and it was not that far and I er came to school -arrived to school the… the first period gone and… and I sawed when the free time, I sawed there was the pants had a little character in here, but there was nothing. It was backwards, so pockets was in the backwards and the little bear character was in the backward and it was like this and nobody said it was turned backward, but I was embarrassing.

I believe there is also the potential to use this activity as an opportunity to assess the listening skills of the other students in the group, by encouraging them to ask questions rather than the questioning being teacher led. Recording the students and making transcripts was time-consuming, but an invaluable professional development exercise that gave me the opportunity to closely analyse the speaking skills of my students. I have also used these recordings to provide EAL training for the Teach First programme within Blaise High School. The trainees are given transcripts and played the recordings and then use the Bell Foundation Assessment Strategy to assess the student's level of English acquisition and set targets for the next steps.

Reference

www.bell-foundation.org.uk/eal-programme/teaching-resources/eal-assessment-framework/

4.3 Building Cohesion in School Through Crafting

Karen Thomas
Manager and Lead Adviser, Portsmouth Ethnic Minority Achievement Service (EMAS)
Rebecca Reeve
EMA Co-ordinator, Miltoncross Academy, Portsmouth, UK

Miltoncross Academy is a large secondary school in inner-city Portsmouth. Until very recently, its pupil population was almost exclusively monolingual White British. However, demographic changes and reduced capacity across the city have meant that the school now has 14% of its pupils who have English as an Additional Language (EAL). Most of the pupils with EAL are new arrivals to the UK, mainly from Europe, and at an early stage of English acquisition. Several refugee and asylum-seeking pupils, some unaccompanied, have also joined the school, and many Roma families in the city choose to send their children to Miltoncross, through 'word of mouth' recommendation.

Miltoncross reacted quickly to this sudden change in cohort and, with EMAS' support, developed effective structures to ensure that pupils with EAL were effectively supported and a small EAL 'department' was born. The EMA Co-ordinator assesses all new arrivals and commissions EMAS' Bilingual Learning Assistants (BLAs) to support curriculum access and family communication through first language. Training for staff in EAL pedagogy remains a vital part of the school's CPD offer. Interventions to support English acquisition are run throughout the week by a part-time teacher of EAL and pastoral support is in place during tailored lunch and homework clubs. The school environment reflects its population and its many diverse languages and cultures are celebrated.

However, beyond the school gates, anti-Roma feeling, which began on social media and quickly turned to adults planning violent protests in the community, threatened to spill into the school. As an immediate and proactive response, Miltoncross decided to use a creative approach to foster cohesion and understanding between the pupils and to create an environment where all students accept each other and value their own and each other's experiences and stories. We chose the 'suitcase' crafting activity as the ideal method for pupils to get to know each other better. Rebecca Reeve remembers:

One of the Year 9 English groups had several of our new arrivals and Roma pupils too, so that was where we started. Our colleagues in the English department were very supportive and keen to develop our activity into a piece of writing. We 'stole' three lessons from them to deliver the activity, plus one additional session after the first lesson with just the new arrivals. We were able to include our EAL Teacher and BLAs in the classroom to support our EAL students.

The 'suitcase' was the metaphor for everything that you bring with you into the class: experiences, hopes, skills, passions – in fact anything that makes you 'you'. We collected pens, glue sticks, scissors, files, card for handles, maps and scores of magazines and had a printer on hand for anything the pupils couldn't find.

In Lesson 1, we talked through what a suitcase might look like for us, in order to start a class discussion, and then the pupils began to create and plan for the next session, so that they had time to collect ideas and images to use. We finished the suitcase in the second session, and some pupils felt able to share theirs with the entire class. Between Lessons 1 and 2, we also organised some focused input for pupils with EAL to practise and support the sharing of the suitcases. We evaluated the sessions together in Lesson 3. Here's what some students said:

What does your suitcase say about you?

'It tells you that's how I feel most days of my life'…'What we are like, think and care about'…'Where I was living before coming to England'

The suitcases were colourful and expressive, some mundane and some insightful, full of aspirations, honesty and good humour. They included home language, culture, 'home' country, hobbies, favourites (food, music, icons).

The outcomes were also immediate and profound. A new arrival from Hungary shared his issues with English acquisition through a BLA. Two English girls sitting behind him were astonished (*'What? No English at all? How does he cope?'*) We explained how to use the BLA, and they included him in their conversations with grace and empathy from then on. English speakers also used the opportunity to share what was important to them. One girl used it to 'come out' and tell the class that she was gay and another, with Tourette's Syndrome, wanted to tell his peers what life was like for him and why he finds behaviour a challenge (*'This colour is anger because people annoy me to see my reactions and it always ends with me hurting them'*).

Some common themes for pupils with EAL emerged. Expectations of education in different countries were frequently discussed (*'It's very different to Chinese schools….It's difficult to say hi, make friends. We think differently, they [English girls] don't think study is quite important'*), as were hugely different life experiences. Pupils shared stories of tigers, bears and bulls on the loose in villages across the world or talked about their love of driving or living in the mountains, a far cry from life in the south of England and the experiences of their peers.

The pupils completely 'got' why they did this activity:

'So that everyone gets to know each other better. It was a good chance to find out about each other'… 'To find out about us, and to help us and others figure out who they are and what they might want to be'

They all enjoyed, or really enjoyed, doing it too (possibly because it wasn't the Shakespeare lessons they were expecting!). There were some issues, however. Some pupils, with fewer life experiences or less maturity, found it difficult to find anything to 'say'. Conversely, some pupils, with lots to share found it hard to find the confidence or the English, or both, to talk about their suitcase, although this was less of a problem in the small group situation. Finally, we need to consider how we roll this out in school next, in an already crowded curriculum.

The benefits for our Year 9 students were clear, however. As one pupil said, *'It's helped us understand others and know more about them and how to help them out'*.

5 Adinkra Creative Links – Music and Textiles in Welcoming Learning Environments

Gameli Tordzro and Naa Densua Tordzro

1 Introduction

This chapter uses a reflexive narrative approach to outline the rationale and overview of working with music and textile to create welcoming learning environments in multiple language and cultural settings for educators and learners and their multiple competencies from their various cultural backgrounds. We reflect on and outline methodological approaches to our interactive African arts practice, that treat Adinkra symbols (Arthur, 2017) from Ghana as creative resource for pupils in primary and secondary schools using textiles, music, creative writing, theatre and storytelling in Glasgow since 2003 (see Figure 5.1 for the Adinkra symbol Adinkrahene). The chapter outlines the background to how we decided to and have used Adinkra symbols as creative resource to deploy the concept of 'treasured opportunities' (Tordzro, 2018) as 'pedagogy of welcome' with teachers in schools attended by 'migrant' children in the UK. It explores identifiable values in pan-African arts practice as language for communicating, teaching and learning; of researching, and as an alternative way of learning to research. We draw on our Ghanaian indigenous knowledge and practices of 'artistic hospitality' for the creation of alternative learning spaces for disadvantaged children and young people. We discuss the idea of creative welcoming, teaching and learning through making art, the processes of creative resistance and well-being, self-worth, displacement and how to be embracing of new teaching and learning environments such as classrooms where migrant children are learners with multiple language and cultural competences. We also reflect on how we used the symbols in an integrated music and textile printing workshop with teachers in Bristol to explore how they could integrate these as a useful and vital teaching resource.

As 'New Scots', our careers as creative artists are responsible for our family successfully emigrating to Scotland. Even though we all spoke and wrote fluent English, when we arrived in Scotland, we encountered a new type of English language – Scots. We realised that within three months, our children had

Figure 5.1 Adinkrahene: The King of all Adinkra symbols. Photograph by Gameli Tordzro

acquired the Scots accent without losing their Ghanaian English accent which they continued to speak at home. We were also aware that the education system was different from Ghana's with the new policy of 'curriculum for excellence'[1] being rolled out in Scotland. As we received requests from schools for arts workshops, we worked together, to initiate a workshop programme for schools and community groups using Adinkra symbols as a creative resource for integrated story, music and textile creation activities – we called it the Adinkra Creative Links. The Creative Links Workshops Program was developed because Gameli encountered Adinkra symbols in the storage of the University of Glasgow Hunterian Museum in 2007. He came across the symbols while researching for a presentation requested by the museum for its celebration of the bicentenary of the abolition of the trans-Atlantic slave trade. Following the presentation, we decided to make Adinkra relevant to our lives as New Scots, taking the opportunity to 'free' the symbols from the 'storage prison' that literally obscured their beauty and value from all Scots. We treasured the opportunity to contribute something substantial to the schools' curriculum. Gameli's concept of 'treasured opportunities' has also been the basis of later developing his work of setting up and directing the Ha Orchestra (Tordzro, 2014). The concept is incorporated into the theoretical drive of all our creative links work which seeks to promote mutual enrichment and cultural exchange. In different learning environments where we have used the concept, we have observed enhanced teaching quality and accelerated learning.[2]

We have illustrated the chapter with Adinkra symbols, as an integral part of its narrative form. As Essel and Opoku Mensah put it, 'The use of a symbol [...] is worth a thousand words' (Essel & Opoku-Mensah, 2014: 31). In her book *Method Meets Art*, Patricia Leavy explores and uncovers how important art-based research is offering researchers resource that exists beyond traditional research and teaching methods.

> It wasn't until I became a mother and a professor that I realized the many ways arts could be harnessed to teach. For example, when my daughter Madeline, was in elementary school and having trouble with geometry, I took her to the Museum of Fine Art in Boston and we analyzed Cubist paintings, looking for shapes. Her geometry improved. (Leavy, 2015: viii)

Leavy asserts that 'the more we understand about human cognition, the clearer it becomes that narrative, stories, and arts can play a major role in teaching diverse subject matters'. Leavy also makes a reference to Pelias' *A Methodology of The Heart: Evoking Academic and Daily Life* drawing our attention to the 'heart' and what matters; '… the heart is never far from what matters' (Pelias, 2004) – which draws our attention to how creative arts practices open spaces that allow new ways of thinking about traditional practices including the spaces we create as educators and how these can be made to be welcoming for learners from diverse backgrounds.

2 Adinkra Symbols: Rationale and Context

Adinkra symbols are a set of symbols with individual names and specific meanings that document the thought, ideology and philosophy of the Akan people of Ivory Coast and Ghana. Traditionally used for textile printing, the actual origins of Adinkra, the creation of the symbols and their usage is very much contested among the Akan people in what has become part of present-day Eastern Cote d'Ivoire, the Western, Bono, Ashanti and Eastern regions of Ghana (Danzy, 2009). However, what Adinkra represents as a symbol system encapsulates more than just a set of motifs for textile design. It is the philosophy of a people, representing an extended body of text, knowledge and understanding of their social, physical and metaphysical worlds (Agbo, 2006).

This is our story of deploying Adinkra symbology as a creative resource and our approach is auto-ethnography; reflecting on how we draw on a hermeneutic[3] (Storey, 1999) process of the Adinkra symbols for textile and music workshops; our joint experience of processes, methods, activities, exploration and discoveries, challenges, knowledge and understanding as well as insight gained together on teaching, learning, creating, researching and engaging with various learning communities. Using the symbols is largely activity based and experiential and so the theoretical underpinnings are steeped in phenomenology – a shared embodied experience in space and time. Our perspective of the Adinkra symbols system for example has changed from a purely conceptual one to an embodied performative perspective as a result of how we encountered and re-engaged with it and began exploring and sharing them, outside our native Ghana, in a growing African diaspora community in Scotland and beyond (see Figure 5.2).

The concept of 'welcome' 'Weozɔ' which means 'welcome' in Gameli's first language Eʋegbe, (translates as 'you have walked' or 'you have travelled') has

Figure 5.2 Symbol: Sankofa retrieve from the past. Be enriched by the value of your history and heritage. Photograph by Gameli Tordzro

implication of the recognition of a person's laboring, tiredness in the body and the need for a rest, refreshment without delay as the first step of a welcome ritual. This means that in the Ewe tradition, welcome is performed as an elaborate social interaction in stages when a person arrives at a specific destination. From that perspective, in our minds, this applies to the presence of Adinkra in the UK. We think it is important to plead your indulgence to allow us to continue our story of how we operationalised using Adinkra in Scotland and why its use permeates our work. Adinkra travelled from Ghana to Scotland before we arrived, but its conditions were basically akin to one who has been displaced and dislocated and as a result lost relevance and value in its new context as a 'foreign' (immigrant, refugee, asylum seeker to borrow some terminologies applied to people) artefact in a museum's locked storage. The normal welcome that should have been accorded such a valuable knowledge system had not been performed. The hospitality it deserved was absent and so its value remained silenced. Therefore, we took on the responsibility of performing the 'Woezɔ' and hosting Adinkra in Scotland and restoring its original dignity by exposing the values it carries. Additionally, we realised that there couldn't be a stronger metaphor to the displacement of some 'migrants' (or 'New Scots' the preferred Scottish government term), and how they have been allocated certain social categories that immediately evoke certain negative connotations that sometimes dehumanise people in the perceptions of the general public – as 'immigrants' 'asylum seekers' and 'refugees' in UK immigration policy. Such categorisation and social tagging mean the immediate loss of certain basic human rights including the right to work and the right to freedom of movement. When we encountered Adinkra symbols in Glasgow, we found them similarly reduced in value and prestige. And so, the decision to liberate the symbols even if not physically, ideologically from the storage context, included the staging of its welcoming: the recognition and acknowledgement of the journeying and arrival in Glasgow and creating the environment for it to thrive and enrich. We saw this not only as an opportunity but a 'treasured opportunity'.

3 Treasured Opportunities

Gameli's theory of treasured opportunities is derived from the idea of enrichment – that when an individual who is disadvantaged with a reduced self-confidence and self-esteem is given the chance to explore possibilities that they never thought could be at their disposal, perceived as an opportunity to transform their life positively, they approach the opportunity with a high level of enthusiasm and sense of dedication, responsibility and focus. In applying this concept to the use of Adinkra symbols, we transferred our own sense of treasuring the opportunity to welcome the Adinkra symbols into our lives in Scotland. We began to introduce and use the symbols and the concept of treasured opportunities in schools and communities we engage with through creative workshop activities. This meant engaging with the symbols at a different level from how we did before in Ghana. We also began incorporating them Naa Densua's textile and fashion work themed on the concept virtues (and named the work as 'Obaa Sima'[4]) – to bring people to encounter and engage with the symbols in an embodied rather than a purely conceptual way. Ultimately, it meant interactions between us and participants, between participants from many different backgrounds and participants and the symbols, but also an introspective interaction of each participant and themselves.

The use of Adinkra symbols to create music and textiles presented the opportunity of different modes of encountering others, relating, creating new knowledge, and understanding, reflecting, discussing, creating new memories and reporting on shared experiences and memories of the process. Thus, the theoretical and methodological thinking behind our Adinkra Creative Links practice is that of phenomenology and reflexive participatory practice. It asks several questions including:

(1) How do we reflect on our life experience through engaging in interactive creative arts activities?
(2) What changes when we engage with others through the language of creative arts?
(3) How do we use arts as the language of education to rediscover and reconstitute our lost and displaced identities and indigenous values in new social contexts?

When we use Adinkra symbols, we introduce them to the group, show them examples of the symbols, their Ghanaian names in Akan[5] and proverbs and adages and how to pronounce the Akan words, and the story or proverb that accompanies the name of the symbol and how it relates to the human experience and the Akan philosophy of life. We invite each participant to explore as many of the symbols as possible and reflect on them and then choose any symbols that resonates their own experience.

Our concerns and interests are in how identities are negotiated at encounters and interactions of new and different people, languages, values and expectations as hosts or guests in new places and spaces – how that affects everyday life experiences; how it is linked to and hinged on education and how education serves everybody irrespective of their backgrounds. We have observed these in the new contexts in which we practice African arts in Scotland and the rest of the UK. We are looking at how the arts is critical in creating inclusive teaching, learning and research environments by placing ourselves in such environments to teach and learn from teaching. Using Adinkra symbols as creative resource, we have worked with teachers, learners, researchers and their research participants to create new opportunities and alternative capabilities for learning, teaching, researching and being actively involved in research as participants. The methods are interactive and exploratory through creative arts activities and their processes. We are also concerned about how teaching, learning and researching become and are perceived not only as creative opportunities but also as 'treasured opportunities' that are welcoming, enriching and promote understanding, positive change and growth for and by migrants and their new host communities.

4 Pedagogy of Welcome and Artistic Hospitality

'You are welcome' is 'Weozɔ' in the Ewe language and can be said as a casual acknowledgement of the arrival of a person or group of persons, but it can also be performed as an elaborate series of activities that draw from what matters to the heart. Welcome can be performed as an embrace and as ongoing continuous embracing. Artistic hospitality is about the comfort and well-being of the guest through knowing the guest as much as it about the host and guest being and or becoming mutually non-judgemental, approachable, affable and compassionate. In a teaching environment, artistic methods and the focus on process interaction and engagement promotes all these values. Lydia Hiorns draws our attention to the performance of artistic hospitality as movement to what is familiar to how we perform we have termed as 'Weoezor'.

> It's often more about the host being known as a good host! The atmosphere created that makes you feel relaxed and welcome depends so much on knowing the guest (will they be uncomfortable if the house is messy? will they be uncomfortable if it's too clean and they are scared of spilling anything?) or being the calm and collected host - the host's spirit pours into whatever they do, if they're thinking about themselves, you can "taste" it... same with if they're thinking about their guests as people to love not reflections or reviews of themselves. (Hiorns, 2012)[6]

In using Adinkra symbols as an integrated multidisciplinary resource in the classroom, a welcoming environment manifests as the classroom is 'dismantled' and rearranged to spread and redirect the gaze and focus from the teacher (as a host) and onto everyone through group interaction, discussion and sharing. In such a situation, which is a fallback to traditional education[7] (Farrant & Farrant, 1980), many barriers to interaction crumble. Even language barriers begin to diminish first because a new language (the language of Adinkra) is ushered in, and everyone is put on the same competency pedestal, second, teacher learner power dynamics move into the arena of creative playfulness, and permitted messiness – it is easy to talk and laugh, and fourthly, the learning process begins to veer into the realm of 'creative interthinking and interthinking creatively' (Fay *et al.*, 2014) between teacher and learner and between learner and learner.

> In collaborative contexts, children bring together an array of perspectives which arise from the diversity of individual histories, experiences, interests, and personalities. Nevertheless, the relationship is conceptualized as being symmetrical, and the goal is to reconcile – share as well as compete – these perspectives to achieve a common learning goal. [...] the togetherness of process is just as important as that of outcome and the collaborative dialogue that mediates the process of interthinking. (Vass *et al.*, 2014)

When we work with Adinkra symbols, our methods are primarily driven by the processes of creative interthinking where we all become hosts and guests to each other.

5 Methodology and Process

The Adinkra textiles printing, music creation and storytelling workshop is an integrated Creative Links workshops we deliver in schools and for community groups as an interlinked series. The workshops activities include researching and identifying Adinkra symbols and their usage, textile printing, story creation, fashion design, garment making and song writing/music making. We engage participants in learning generally about the Adinkra symbols and how they carry coded meaning in Ghanaian culture. We encourage participants to self-explore the symbols on printed cards and or printed fabric and from online resources (Tordzro, 2019a). We encourage participants to work in groups or independently to choose a symbol for discussion. The discussion generates words, idioms and expressions in how the symbols resonate with each participant or the group they work in.

The material generated from the discussion become material for a creative piece, a poem, song, story or a new proverb. The physical symbols we use in our workshops are on print-screen for printing and print-stamps carved out of broken calabash (see Figure 5.3). The participants dip their stamps in paint and press onto cotton to leave and imprint. The process works at multiple levels: from introducing participants to a cultural heritage in Ghana, indirectly opening up possibilities for them to reflect on their own cultural heritage and beliefs; to allow participants to experience the aesthetic of working with materials (paints of rich natural colours,

Figure 5.3 Adinkra print stamps made from pieces of broken calabash. Photograph by Gameli Tordzro

screen printing, calabash stamps made in Ghana, cotton bags, aprons and T-shirts onto which participants print their Adinkra symbols) and to engage and enjoin participants in a creative arts process in a non-threatening, open and welcoming environment for all participants regardless of their background (from refugees, asylum seekers to vulnerable young and old people) in the community. The workshop environment is important because it is not only about teaching how to do Adinkra prints and create stories and songs, but it is also about learning new things, sharing values; how the symbols and the process of the activity creates meaning and resonates with other aesthetic linguistic and social experiences. It is also about the sense of achievement in a short period of time; the songs, prints, stories created and co-created by the participants. At the core of all that is the value of art and therapy (Wigram *et al.*, 1995) and derived from interactive engagement, care, compassion and well-being between all participants and how that is a shared experience in a friendly and safe environment. Adinkra symbols as a multimodal and communication medium allows new multilingual and human relationships to emerge and flourish.

6 Co-creation: Music

In discussing each symbol with participants, we explore their communicative values, affordances and usage for 'languaging' (Phipps, 2007) and translating cultures (Levine & Phipps, 2012) into the relevant contemporary contexts of our workshop and research participants. For example, symbols like 'Funtunfunefu' and 'Bi nka bi' (see Figure 5.4) communicate specific concepts of care, sharing, shared ownership and courtesy (Tordzro, 2019b). And so, in discussing them, we

Figure 5.4 Symbol: Bi Nka Bi printed on textile (may no one bite the another). Photograph by Gameli Tordzro

generate words that can become the resource for poems, stories and songs with questions like:

- How does a symbol transform into a poem?
- How does the poem become a song?
- How is a song composed and performed?
- Can the process be captured and shared?

Funtunfunefu Denkyemfunefu

The answers to these questions create a pathway to interaction, engagement and participation. Participation can be for various purposes and yield varied results for participant, researcher and practitioner alike. In exploring the sound of the name of a symbol like Funtunfunefu, a group can be taken through the following steps:

Step 1. Exploring Rhythm: *'Fùn tùn fù né - fù (-pause-) Dén kyém fù né - fù' (using the accents for change in tones spaces for rhythm)*

For example, the name of the conjoined crocodile is a penta-syllabic one. The alternating low and high accents of the name of the symbols can be played rhythmically on any percussive instrument with low and high pitch options like a djembe drum or sogo, kpanlogo or apentema drum.

Step 2. Exploring Lyrics Creation

The words generated by the discussion of the symbol is then arranged into a co-created symbol, rhythm and tone come immediately into play and create the basis of

Figure 5.5 Funtunfunefu: Designed in Kente textile and represented by Senanu Adzo Tordzro

a music making opportunity. A poem can be converted into a song. The adage that accompanies Funtunfunefu means 'two crocodiles share the same stomach but they fight over food' (see Figure 5.5).

'Denkyem abienu tua aforo bako, nanso wodidi a woko'

Becomes the basis of the lyrics.

Step 3. Creating the Melody
Once the group comes up with up to five lyrical lines, the lines can be put to a tune, either by singing each line sequentially by voice, or the tune is created and played on an instrument and repeated vocally by the participants individually or as a group until a full tune emerges.

Step 4. Sharing
This activity can be planned and carried out either as a breakout individual or group activity. At the end of this activity, the poem/song becomes a major significant output, the experience of which is mutually owned and shared by all participants. If there is scope, the piece can be performed in front of an audience.

7 Adinkra Textile Printing

Step 1. After warmly welcoming participants, the workshop facilitator gives a brief history of the Adinkra symbols, their origin, meaning and usefulness in society. In explaining the history behind the symbols, various visual means are used teaching and showing the participants about the symbols. The use of computers, cards and the physical symbols of the Adinkra stamps are used in the workshop.

Step 2. The participants encouraged to touch the symbols, read, think and talk amongst each other about the symbols and how they relate to them.

Step 3. Based on what they have explored about the symbols, the participants are then invited to choose a symbol with a meaning that resonates with an important aspect of their lives (see Figure 5.6). They are asked to share with the group (if they wish) the reason for their choice of symbol.

Step 4. In the next stage, each participant selects a corresponding stamp or print-screen and a paint colour with which to stamp, and then print the stamp onto their cream cotton bag or piece of cloth or T-shirt. The colours of the paints and the meaning of the symbols allow the participants to express themselves, and their feelings about who they are and their place in the world.

Step 5. The workshop facilitator then shows them how the printing is done and then leaves them to print the symbol(s) of their choice. We encourage participants to create pieces, especially in textile printing as souvenir to take home, also display at schools (see Figure 5.7).

Step 6. The printed symbols are put on display

Figure 5.6 An original Adinkra textile. Photograph by Gameli Tordzro
Cloth donated to Naa Densua and Gameli by Jan Sutch Picard a Scottish storyteller in Iona

Figure 5.7 Adinkra-print cotton bag an output of an Adinkra printing workshop activity. Photograph by Gameli Tordzro

8 Conclusion

The idea behind the creative links workshops is also to integrate the various creative arts workshop activities in a way that makes the activities relevant to the learning context in relation to a particular lesson. For example, in a climate change lesson, the class can explore creating a song that tells a story, with key words drawn from a chosen symbol that shines a light on a particular aspect of the problem. This can be the habits that affect the climate, the manifestation and the effect on life, or the solution and how that would look like. So, the class can create a new story, in which there is a song, poetry and proverbs drawing on inspiration from a single or a selection of symbols that can be printed on a backdrop textile or costume (e.g. T-shirt). This brings up the question and concerns regarding and around cultural appropriation in the usage of Adinkra symbols.

We will not define 'cultural appropriation' as there is already ample text on the subject. We will deal with this briefly only in response to teachers' discomfort about using culturally charged resources when they are not well steeped in the culture themselves. Again, this problem rather presents many treasurable opportunities including making the learning space and lessons memorable ones by bringing in facilitators like ourselves who are well versed in the symbols. Where that is difficult because of budget and other constraints, it is an opportunity not only for the teacher but the whole class to research and present to each other – learning in collaboration.

Even though Adinkra symbols are protected by the folklore intellectual property laws of Ghana, teaching the symbols through usage in the classroom is not an infringement on the law. Moreover, the symbols are presented in a variety of books and in the public domain online on various websites. In our view in the context of education, where various cultures intersect, it is rather a healthy and welcoming act to bring important and valuable cultural experiences to bear on the interactive activities of the classroom if it is not to the detriment of the cultural values the symbols hold especially for those who uphold the traditions and their associated languages. The original purpose and usage of Adinkra symbols include how they can help to forge new connections, understandings, relationships, experiences and a new sense of belonging, for everyone involved.

When we use Adinkra symbols in our work, they engender shared smiles, warm tones and friendly dispositions, and easily, feelings of awkwardness or shyness that we shared initially were soon dispelled through the physical experience of expressing our beliefs and feelings through the stamps or screen printing and colours (of the paint), and through interactions with one another. The open and welcoming environment creates a relaxing atmosphere for participants to be themselves and enjoy the opportunity to communicate with others, no matter how little they understand each other's language. It is also a space where people connect and informally learn a few words and speak in English with the people they meet.

Throughout our work in the communities and schools, we have realised and identified that children and adults are very interested in the Adinkra textile printing, particularly because of the instant results they achieve from participating. I realised that no matter where the Adinkra symbols printing workshop is done, the response and reaction is almost the same. It does not matter whether we understood each other language-wise. In the end the symbols, the bags and the paint become our language, our tool of communication in the gathering or space. We encourage participants to create pieces especially in textile printing as a souvenir to take home, also to display in schools. The participants leave feeling very happy and content with what they have achieved within a very short time, and they have something to remind them of their time spent at the workshop. The space becomes a place where new friendships are formed and stories are shared between participants about themselves and their home countries. We ask questions like: 'How would our workshop participant value an apron they made and printed themselves, against one she buys from the shop?'

Gameli's concept of 'Treasured Opportunity' his music, and storytelling practice, and Naa Densua's fashion and textile practice skills were used to develop a creative arts way of working across disciplines in a manner that linked textile printing, story creation and song creation (Textile, Music and Literary Arts) using Adinkra symbols in an interdisciplinary manner for learners of all ages. As we continue to develop this practice and the value it creates for us and those we engage with, we observe how we have and continue to communicate through combined arts practice both in the pan-African diaspora context in Scotland, and how recently we have begun to transfer the experience, knowledge and skills back to Ghana in contemporary and indigenous contexts of applied interdisciplinary practice of arts, social research, global education based on the idea of functional quality education for everybody on the planet. Our methodological approaches stem from embodied non-formal interactive teaching and learning traditions of African communities. We have applied our storytelling skills to bring a narrative approach to our reflections.

Notes

(1) Curriculum for Excellence: 'As part of their learner journey, all children and young people in Scotland are entitled to experience a coherent curriculum from 3 to 18, in order that they have opportunities to develop the knowledge, skills and attributes they need to adapt, think critically and flourish in today's world'. https://education.gov.scot/
(2) Examples of this are represented in The Adinkra Poetry Series, including the following volumes Funtumfunefu 'Synched' Aya 'The Resilient', and Ancetral Code. See https://adinkralinks.net/book-series
(3) Hermeneutics: The theory of interpretation. Storey (1999) draws attention to how in his *Truth and Methods*, German philosopher Hans-Georg Gadamer argues that 'an understanding of a cultural text is always from the perspective of one who understands' (1999: 61).
(4) Obaa Sima means 'virtuous woman' in Akan. In most African cultures, womanhood is revered as vital to fertility, continuity and the sustainable development of society. In Ewegbe, for example, the word for woman is 'Nyɔnu' from and stands for that which makes all become good.
(5) The Akan are a sub-Saharan meta-ethnicity in what became split between French and English colonialist times into what is now parts of Côte d'Ivoire and Ghana. It is a multidialectal group, including Twi, Fante, Asante, Akwapim, Kwawu, Bono, Akyem, Agona, Sefwi and Wassa.
(6) Artistic Hospitality: http://lydiahiorns.co.uk/blog/2017/07/19/breathing-artistic-hospitality/
(7) Traditional Education: According to Farrant, 'Traditional education is different in many ways from modern education. […] is a community responsibility and uses the child's work experience' (1980: 30).

References

Agbo, A.H. (2006) *Values of Adinkra and Agama Symbols* Kumasi, Ghana: Bigshy Designs and Publications.
Arthur, K.G.F. (2017) *Cloth as Metaphor (Re)reading the Adinkra Cloth Symbols of the Akan of Ghana* (2nd edn). Bloomington, IN: iUniverse Books.
Danzy, J. (2009) *Adinkra Symbols: An Ideographic Writing System* PhD Thesis [online]. Stony Brook University. Available from: https://repo.library.stonybrook.edu/xmlui/handle/11401/72101?show=full [Accessed 23 February 2022] .
Essel, O. and Opoku-Mensah, I. (2014) Pan-African artistic reflections in Kwame Nkrumah Memorial Park. *International Journal of African Society Cultures and Traditions* 1 (2), 33–40.
Farrant, J.S. (1980) *Principles and Practice of Education* (new edn). London: Longman.
Fay, R., Andrews, J., Frimberger, K. and Tordzro, G. (2014) *Creative Interthinking, Interthinking Creatively*. Glasgow, UK: University of Glasgow School of Education. See RM Borders, researching-multilingually-at-borders.com (accessed June 2020).
Hiorns, L. (2012) Breathing artistic hospitality. See http://lydiahiorns.co.uk/blog/2017/07/19/breathing-artistic-hospitality/ (February 2022).
Leavy, P. (2015) *Method Meets Art: Arts-Based Research Practice* (2nd edn.) New York: Guildford Press.
Levine, G.S. and Phipps, A. (2012) *Critical and Intercultural Theory and Language Pedagogy. AAUSC Issues in Language Program Direction*. Boston, MA: Heinle Cengage Learning.
Pelias, R.J. (2004) *A Methodology of the Heart: Evoking Academic and Daily Life*. Walnut Creek, CA: Oxford: AltaMira Press.
Phipps, A. (2007) *Learning the Arts of Linguistic Survival: Languaging, Tourism, Life.* (p. 205). Clevedon: Channel View Publications.
Phipps, A.M. and Kay, R. (2016) *Languages in Migratory Settings: Place, Politics, and Aesthetics*. Abingdon: Routledge.

Storey, J. (1999) *Cultural Consumption and Everyday Life. Cultural Studies in Practice*. New York: Oxford University Press.
Tordzro, G. (2019a) *AdinkraLinks International Poetry Network*. Glasgow: Adinkra Links Network. See https://adinkralinks.net (accessed July 2020).
Tordzro, G.K. (2014) *Ha Orchestra Website The Scottish African Symphonic Orchestra*. Glasgow: Gameli Tordzro. See http://www.haorchestra.com (accessed March 2020).
Tordzro, G.K. (2018) *Story Storying and Storytelling; A Reflection on Documentary Film, Music and Theatre as Creative Arts Research Practice*. PhD Creative Arts Production Practice Based Reflection, University of Glasgow, Glasgow [Online]. See http://theses.gla.ac.uk/8941/1/2017Tordzrophd.pdf (accessed November 2019).
Tordzro, G.K. (ed.) (2019b) *Funtunfunefu 'Synched'* (1st edn). Glasgow: Meli Creatives Publishing.
Vass, E., Karen, L., Jones, A. and Miell, D. (2014) The affectively constituted dimensions of creative interthinking. *International Journal of Education Research* 66, 63–77.
Wigram, T., Saperston, B. and West, R. (1995) *The Art and Science of Music Therapy: A Handbook*. London: Harwood Academic Publishers.

5.1 Working With Adinkra Symbols and Printing – Unlocking Creativity in Children

Alison Grotzke
Wheatfield Primary School, Bradley Stoke, Bristol, UK

1 Context

The old English proverb, 'A picture is worth a thousand words', teaches us that more information can be understood from a single picture than from a written description. Therefore, when supporting the language development of our children, it's no surprise that visuals, such as symbols, are used in schools to capture attention, inspire interaction and stimulate learning. Children learning language, such as children developing EAL, respond positively to visuals because they break down those barriers to communication. They can be highly emotive and instantly recognisable which helps children to make sense of the message being conveyed and in return they can use them to represent their own thoughts, even if they aren't able to use a language fluently.

As an EAL teaching assistant at Wheatfield Primary School in Bristol, the use of visuals is integral to my role. Celebrating its 20th anniversary this year, my school is a thriving, multi-cultural community with around 400 pupils aged 4–11 and 50 staff. With 32% of children developing EAL registered, Wheatfield works hard to ensure that our children from all over the world can access the curriculum, enjoy school life and reach their goals. Most importantly, children are encouraged to embrace diversity and understand that bilingualism is an asset to be proud of.

2 Rationale

The idea for working with symbols creatively was inspired by a workshop I attended which introduced me to African Adinkra symbols and printing them onto textiles which looked really interesting and fun. I particularly liked the positive messages connected with the symbols, such as bravery and hope, and I knew they would evoke emotional responses as well as help instigate conversation. I was keen to introduce aspects of the workshop so that the children could try something new and learn about another culture in the process. One area of our curriculum covers 'Understanding the World', where the children have time to ask questions and show curiosity with the world around them. As such it was important to me that the children and I talked through the Adinkra symbols, where they came from and their meanings. We saw this as a 'treasured opportunity' which is discussed by Tordzro and Tordzo (Chapter 5, this volume). We also looked at how the symbols are printed onto fabric by the people of Ghana but also how they are becoming more visible on items such as T-shirts, water bottles and jewellery. Exploring the cultural origins of the Adinkra symbols was a key part of the process set out here in this chapter, and I recommend other readers to do the same if they decide to explore Adinkra symbols in their creative work with language learners.

I realised that an activity like this would also be a useful addition to my otherwise very target driven intervention. In school, I'm mindful that language demands can be overwhelming for EAL children as they are constantly bombarded with information and at times they just need to zone out for a moment while they process everything. Therefore, any opportunities to express themselves creatively is valuable because they can have a break from concentrating hard and just enjoy being in the moment, letting their feelings flow. I find sessions like these can really help children open up and make a connection with you, which then consequently helps with moving their learning forward.

3 Activity

In order to bring the symbols and their meanings alive for the children, I found examples on the internet and chose an appropriate selection which I printed out, laminated and turned into flashcards. I managed to find a company which sold ready-made rubber stamps and then I glued them with a Pritt Stick onto clear plastic positioning blocks. Once corks were glued on as handles, they were ready to go. The ink needed to be as mess free as possible so I bought inexpensive black ink pads from a local craft store. I pre-cut the card and fabric, sourced from our art cupboard, into manageable sizes and drew guidelines. Several children, from Years 3 to 6 (ages 7 to 11), took part in the sessions. First, I introduced the symbols and their place in African culture. We discussed meanings, the designs themselves and selected which ones appealed and why. During the next session, the children were able to see photos of the symbols on clothing and put them into context before creating their own designs.

4 How It Went

In practice, the sessions worked well, especially when I mentioned the word 'display' and explained that their work would be on show for all to admire. This created a real buzz in the air, and the children were itching to get going. It was amazing to see how intrigued the children were as they studied the flashcards and interpreted them with their own points of view. The power of symbols is well known, and the children found the flashcards fascinating, even funny at times. They unlocked a sense of freedom, and the older children really enjoyed inventing their own symbols and possible meanings. When printing, the children had to use care and skill to place their stamps accurately to ensure the best quality. I could see that they were working

Figure 5.1.1 Our school display

out how best to apply themselves in order to improve their technique, often wanting to have another go. I was amazed at how inventive they were; one of the children decided to make a bookmark.

One morning after the display went up (see Figure 5.1.1), it was very rewarding to overhear a reception parent appreciate the children's work as she pointed out the symbols to her child. They obviously resonated with her as she excitedly explained what they were.

5 My Reflections

Since the first sessions, I have reflected on their value and believe that the children benefited in many ways. The children had space to engage as much or as little as they wanted without any pressure. One thoughtful Year 6 pupil, sent over to live with a relative after witnessing the destruction of his home due to Hurricane Irma, set quietly about his artwork, keeping talk to a minimum. But that was okay; he joined in and allowed himself to create something he was clearly pleased with. I felt the activity had a healing nature to it and empowered the children to become more confident. In Figure 5.1.2 you can see some of the children's comments about the Adinkra symbols they explored in the session.

Friendship	Learn from your mistakes	Strength	Forgiveness
It looks like two loaves of bread 	I like this as it has swirls and I like art 	I like this because it's got muscles 	This one looks like a butterfly 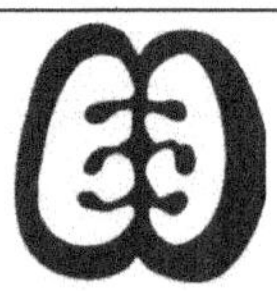

Figure 5.1.2 Some of the children's comments about the Adinkra symbols we used

Practically, because it's mess free, the activity is suitable for all ages and quick to set up. I chose coloured card in vibrant colours, but of course, there is no end to how this can be adapted. Next time, I want to use different colour ink pads and fabric paint so that the children can bring in a plain T-shirt to print onto. I also thought about introducing clay or plasticine as an alternative to card and fabric. The clay can harden and with a hole could even be made into pendants.

5.2 A School Radio Station

Dominique Moore
Local Authority Advisor, Ethnic Minority and Traveller Achievement Service, South Gloucestershire, UK

One summer in the early 2000s, I was working as a teacher with the Ethnic Minority Achievement Service in Bristol providing additional support to BAME pupils in one of the city's diverse primary schools. In the classroom, I always endeavoured to use resources that affirmed the pupils' cultural backgrounds. I wanted to take this idea and replicate it outside of the classroom. I had a strong interest in music, including music from around the world. I often played music in the classroom, calm music with a tempo slower than the heartbeat when practising a skill just taught or more up-tempo music at the end of the lesson to signal time to finish and tidy up. I used a wide range of music including music from the pupils' cultural heritage. Much of the music played was unfamiliar, but they showed recognition and said they enjoyed hearing music they might have heard in the home, sometimes describing it as the music their parents listened to. I knew the pupils also enjoyed the pop music of the time.

Seeing the positive impact of the music, I thought I would try setting up a school radio station. I sought and got the approval of the headteacher and brought equipment into school for the radio station. I introduced the idea to pupils in a Key Stage 2 assembly, explaining that the radio station would broadcast music into the playground at lunchtimes and at the end of the school day. At the end of the day, there would also be announcements for parents and pupils, for example, to remind pupils about after-school clubs, reminding them to bring swimming kit the next day or to remind parents of school trips and payment deadlines.

The idea created a bit of a buzz in the assembly. I explained that there would be different jobs: managers, technicians and presenters. I explained each role; managers to run the station, for example, choosing who was presenting and when, ensuring everything was run smoothly; technicians would set up and take down the equipment and be there with the presenter during their show; presenters to select music, chat between tracks and make announcements. I informed the pupils that they would have to apply for the jobs and that a form would be provided for anyone who wanted to apply for one of the roles. I added that we would not just be using English but would encourage the use of children's other languages by the presenters. I also informed them that knowledge of different types of music would also be very welcome; I listed some of the types of music I knew were known to many of the pupils.

I said that the ability to speak another language or know about different types of music was not essential, but very welcome.

I had a lot of pupils come up to me after the assembly expressing a strong interest in the project. Many of the application forms were taken and completed for all roles. There were so many applications that there was a great choice of pupils to choose from. Those who were bilingual (or multilingual) or had knowledge of a range of musical styles made this clear in their applications. I selected three managers first, so they could be involved in the process of selecting pupils for the other roles. Some of the shyer students chose to apply for the role of technicians or managers. Several of the presenters selected were bilingual, the managers and the technicians included pupils who were bilingual and happy to share knowledge of various types of music. It was a good team that reflected the diversity of the school.

The broadcasting used two fairly powerful speakers and an amplifier, a mixer and two of the schools CD/cassette players and a microphone and microphone stand. The radio was broadcast from the Year 6 classroom that had a good view onto the playground. At each broadcast, the technicians set up the radio placing the speakers in the playground, wires coming through the window. The presenters stood in the classroom in a position where they had a good view of the playground.

I had been unsure how well it would work and how the lunchtime supervisors would react, even they had been informed! Luckily it was during a hot summer term, and it worked out better than I could have imagined.

The presenters had been selected because of their confidence in speaking to large groups of pupils. Those who were bilingual switched easily between English and their first languages chatting between songs, joining in with the lyrics and interacting with the pupils in the playground. The choice of music played was predominantly current pop music but included music reflecting the diversity of the school population.

When broadcasting at the end of the day, it was mostly announcements, and the presenters were very good at communicating messages to parents in English and in a range of the school's languages. It was evident from parents' reactions and comments that they liked and found the announcements useful.

Some of the highlights of the radio station were seeing nearly all the Key Stage 1 pupils filling the area of playground close to the speakers singing loudly, waving their arms in the air and dancing to 'Bob the Builder Can We Fix It?', in unison, under the instructions of the presenters. It was one of the most requested songs by the younger pupils.

Similarly, another song that regularly filled the playground was Lou Bega's 'Mambo No 5'. The pupils were very familiar with the lyrics and the dance moves. It was a real pleasure seeing so many pupils dancing joyously together in the playground. When there were songs that attracted groups of pupils to come and dance together, the presenters became skilled at encouraging the dancers, praising their moves, calling out their names often switching between English and their first languages. This often encouraged others to come and join in.

At the summer school fair, a PA system was hired, and the parents running the fair asked some of the radio's presenters to help out with announcements, describing stalls, what they offered, and encouraging people to come and have a look and buy things. One of the pupils most at ease with using her home language really shone on that day. She was so confident, cheerful and clear in her announcements in English and Punjabi. She received a lot of praise from parents and staff.

The use of parents' and children's first languages was appreciated and valued, including by parents. The school was already valued in its community, and diversity was seen as one of the school's strengths and was celebrated by all. So, this project added to the schools' positive reputation. When my placement at the school ended, I was really pleased to be approached by the lunchtime supervision staff. They requested that the radio station continue after I left not only because they enjoyed the music but also describing the impact on the pupils, how they enjoyed it. They also emphasised the positive impact on behaviour in the playground.

For readers who would like to know more of the technical details, this next section explains more about the equipment, set up and practical matters. I provided a budget mixer, used by DJs, with a cross fader and microphone input plug and two auxiliary input sockets.

I used two school CD players connected to the mixer via the headphone sockets; these were used to play the CDs. As noted earlier, I provided a microphone and microphone stand. The microphone was also plugged into the mixer, and I supplied a simple amplifier and a pair of speakers with long leads. The amplifier and speakers were powerful enough to be heard throughout the playground.

The equipment was kept on a wheeled trolley; at break times when the radio was functioning, the speakers were connected to the amplifier and lowered into the playground through the classroom window. The presenters could stand by the window with a clear view into the playground. The pupil with the job of technician was responsible for setting up the equipment and packing it up. They also had to be present throughout the broadcast to support the presenter who selected the songs, place them in the CD player and control the music and microphone volume via the mixer. The mixer allowed songs to be played seamlessly with no pause between each song and permitted the presenter to speak over the music while it was playing or to sing along with tunes. The students with the jobs of managers were responsible for drawing up rotas of presenters and technicians for each broadcast, and one of the managers was also expected to be present for each broadcast.

In the next school I worked in, I also set up a radio station with similar impact. An encouraging message was relayed to me after I left that school. During their school fair, they played some of the music I had left with the school over the PA system. It included a song that had been very popular across North Africa 'Ya Rayah'. A family had very recently arrived in Britain from Tunisia. The fair was the first school event they had attended as a family. Hearing 'Ya Rayah' playing over the speakers had such a positive impact on the parent that she felt compelled to approach the headteacher saying how the song had been very popular in Tunisia and hearing it at the school had moved her and made her feel very welcomed.

It is widely accepted that representation matters for students; seeing themselves represented in the curriculum and in the resources used to deliver the curriculum promotes a sense of belonging and contributes to well-being and improved attainment. In conclusion, there can be benefits to extending cultural inclusiveness to outside the classroom.

Further reading

Dr S. Themelis and B. Foster "Education for Roma: the potential of inclusive, curriculum-based innovation to improve learning outcomes." Background paper prepared for the Education for All Global Monitoring Report 2013/4. Teaching and learning: Achieving quality for all. See https://citeseerx.ist.psu.edu/viewdoc/download?doi=10.1.1.739.3124&rep=rep1&type=pdf

5.3 Singing Songs From Jamaica in Early Years Settings and Primary Schools in South Gloucestershire

Lois Francis
Local Authority Advisor, Ethnic Minority Achievement Service, South Gloucestershire, UK

1 Context for These Activities

South Gloucestershire is a mixed urban and rural area. The council has a small but growing number of minority ethnic residents. The 2011 Census reported that 5% of the population is made of up of members of minority ethnic communities (compared to the average of 14% for England and Wales). In addition, 2.5% of the population is classified as 'White Other' (from South Gloucestershire Council website). In some areas, there is little cultural diversity, and many children living in the Local Authority may not have opportunity to interact or liaise with someone from another cultural group. All children, however, need to be prepared for life in a diverse society, a society which is multicultural and multilingual. Early years settings and schools need to be proactive in providing experiences which are culturally diverse if they are to fulfil their role in developing the whole child and broadening children's understanding of the world. Providing opportunities for staff and pupils to enjoy songs and playground action songs from Jamaica would be a way of helping settings and schools to fulfil this very important role. Below is an outline of how this has been done in early years settings and schools. It is hoped that the ideas presented can be replicated by those working in settings and schools to help to broaden children's experiences.

The aims of using Jamaican songs and rhymes were to:

- contribute to creating a welcoming environment for pupils from diverse backgrounds;
- promote an inclusive ethos in the setting or school so that all children have a sense of belonging;
- give recognition of the culture of children from African/Caribbean background and so increase self-esteem and motivation;
- provide opportunity for African/Caribbean pupils to learn songs from their culture;
- help to prepare all children for life in a diverse society;

- foster respect for people of other backgrounds and
- provide enjoyment and fun.

The activities were done in two ways:

- Cluster training for staff in early years settings and training for staff in primary schools. Staff were taught the songs and actions so that they could use them in settings or schools. All the words of the songs were provided for staff.
- Whole-class workshops with children in primary schools and in a special school during Black History Month activities. Songs were also included in Jamaican food and culture activities and when sharing stories from the Caribbean. Children were taught the songs and the actions.

The songs and action songs from Jamaica used were:

Water come a mi eye – A song about someone remembering Liza. When he does, he says, 'Water come a mi eye'. The song is sung with enthusiasm. It provides opportunity to dance in many different ways. The song can be found on this link.

https://www.mamalisa.com/?t=es&p=5663

Linstead Market – A Jamaican folk song about a mother who goes to the market to sell her ackee fruit. Unfortunately, she does not sell any, and so her children will go hungry. Ackee is a famous fruit in Jamaica, and ackee mixed with salt fish (dried fish) is its national dish. This song is lively, and participants have the opportunity to do a variety of movements to match the rhythm of the song, e.g. snapping the finger, clapping, tapping the feet. Other actions done show how the woman is feeling, e.g. spreading arms wide to express how she feels about having no food or a hand on the jaw to express her sadness. An example of the song being sung can be found on the following links:

https://www.youtube.com/watch?v=KdbSN4wfSfo
https://www.mamalisa.com/?t=es&p=2857
https://www.youtube.com/watch?v=ICstpeu4Oes

Punchinella – This is a playground ring game song. Punchinella stands in the middle and does an action as the others sing, 'What can you do Punchinella little fella?' Everyone joins in with the action and sing, 'We can do it too!' Punchinella then chooses someone to come into the ring and be Punchinella. The song then starts all over again and keeps going until all the participants are chosen or there is no more time to play! The song and actions can be enjoyed from this link:

https://www.youtube.com/watch?v=PoF7plxr3RU

Little Sally Walker – This is a lovely song for younger children. Children stand in a ring with Sally in the middle looking sad. She can be rubbing her eyes or wiping tears away. Those in the ring sing and clap and encourage Sally to, 'Rise and wipe your weeping eyes'. Sally is told in the song to, 'Turn to the east, turn to the west, turn to the one you love the best'. At this point, she chooses someone to be Sally and the game starts again as shown on this link:

> https://makingmusicfun.net/htm/f_mmf_music_library_songbook/little-sally-walker-lyrics.php

School subjects/topics which were covered or could be covered by the activities:

Understanding the world and geography – pupils looked at the world map to find Jamaica and its location in relation to the UK. They had to think of how to travel, e.g. mode of transport and what ocean they would go across. Additional work on geography could also be done through the song 'Little Sally Walker'. In this song, children could learn the compass positions of east and west.

Aspects of personal, social, health and economic education (PSHE) were also covered as children had to work together in singing the songs, doing the actions and taking turns. They also had opportunity to make personal choice, for example, in the Punchinella playground song, where children had to decide on their own actions which the others then had to join in and do. The songs also helped to show similarities and differences around the world. These activities can show children that other children sing songs and do actions in their parts of the world. As some of the songs were sung in Jamaican Creole, e.g. 'Water come a mi eye', this also showed children that people speak in different ways and that there are different dialects of English.

Music and dance is an obvious area covered. The songs lend themselves easily to thinking about different musical rhythms and particularly rhythms associated with the Caribbean islands. Actions from the songs could be used as part of PE and dance, especially the warming up aspects. The activities could be extended by accompanying the songs with percussion instruments. Some drums or shakers might work well.

The sessions were generally fun and enjoyed by all. Adults were willing to participate in the singing and actions during the training sessions or staff meetings. In the work with children, some preferred to join in the actions of others, for example, in the Punchinella song, more than doing an individual action. One way of encouraging all children to participate would be to have two children working together on an action.

Although it is difficult to assess the impact of these activities as they were done as one off activities, it is hoped that the schools in which they were done will continue to do them. It is also hoped that the schools will extend the activities as part of their promotion of cultural diversity in the curriculum.

Other websites, apart from the ones shown above, to support these activities:
Mama Lisa's World: International Music and Culture

> https://www.mamalisa.com/?t=ec&c=113

> (Select appropriate verses for the songs)

> YouTube videos, e.g. https://www.youtube.com/user/JamaicanKidsSongs?app=desktop (Choose appropriate songs)

Children song books, e.g. Jamaican Folk Songs by Louise Bennett

https://www.amazon.co.uk/Jamaican-Folk-Songs-Louise-Bennett/dp/B00242W47O

If a school is interested in doing these activities, a good resource would be to invite a member of the Jamaican community to visit the school and teach the songs.

This article is written as an example of activities provided for schools by the Ethnic Minority and Traveller Achievement Service, Integra Schools, South Gloucestershire. For more information and guidance, visit https://www.integra.co.uk/.

5.4 Audio in School – School Languages on the Tannoy System

Judith Prosser

In 2018, I was teaching in a large ethnically diverse secondary school, where more than 40% of the pupils were recorded as having English as an Additional Language (EAL). The school had a wide catchment area that encompassed students from affluent families, who lived nearby in the grand houses on the leafy streets, then gradually extended out to include the inner-city areas that had more affordable housing; the students from these areas commuted by local train or bus each day. The majority of the EAL students came from the more economically deprived areas of the city, but despite this lack of social equality, the school had an atmosphere that could be compared to a melting pot, where diversity was not just occasionally celebrated, but accepted as the norm. When on breaktime duty, one would regularly hear students readily swapping between their home languages and English. At that time, there were at least 40 different languages spoken by the students and staff at the school; the largest student language group was Somali, then Arabic and Punjabi. Anecdotally, many of the white middle-class parents were drawn to the school not only for its reputation for good academic standards and long-standing reputation for excellence in the teaching in art, music and drama, but its ethnic and cultural diversity. However, even in a school with such an inclusive ethos, there was a sense that some students perceived that a hierarchy of languages existed and that English was the most important and the benefits of bilingualism would only come from learning the modern foreign languages that are a part of the English school curriculum.

Even in an enlightened school with such an inclusive ethos, some students were still reluctant to use their home language. UNESCO's Mother Languages Day presented an opportunity to raise the profile of bilingualism and celebrate the impressive range of languages spoken by the students.

The school had just acquired a state-of-the-art tannoy system, which could be programmed to play pre-recorded messages and was capable of broadcasting into all the classrooms and offices in the building. In consultation with staff and students, it was decided to teach the whole school some multilingual greetings. Before this, the tannoy had only been used by staff for communicating essential information, or to signal the end of lessons with a jingle; the sound of student voices would be a sharp contrast that would make everyone stop and listen. The recorded greetings were to be broadcast during the morning and afternoon tutor sessions, for instance,

> 'The school language of the day is Somali: Good morning -Subax Wanagsaan' (repeat).
> 'The school language of the day is Somali: Good afternoon -Galab Wanagsaan' (repeat).

The greetings were recorded on an iPhone during an hour-long group session. It took about 30 minutes to make four recordings, but it was necessary to prepare the students beforehand, in the way one would do for any speaking lesson by modelling intonation, volume and pace of delivery. Participation in the recordings was voluntary, and it was a group decision that the broadcasters would remain anonymous.

The recording activity was a great opportunity for students to practise and extend their English-speaking skills as they held animated discussions about the differences and similarities of the same greetings in their home languages. Cultural differences also came to light, for instance, when two students informed us that 'good afternoon' is not a usual greeting in Korean or Punjabi and so in this case we settled for 'Have a good day' and 'Hello', respectively. The recording process also provided an opportunity for the students to adopt the role of teacher; it was a joy to hear students using technical teaching vocabulary to improve intonation and pace of the delivery of the greetings.

Initially, the project only involved the students at the early stages of English language acquisition, but the word had spread, and the response was so positive from our advanced EAL students that the event was now set to become Mother Languages Fortnight. The project could have run for longer, but it was decided that momentum would eventually be lost, and other opportunities to showcase the other 30 plus languages spoken in the school should be found. Just in case of any technical issues, the recordings were sent to the school's IT team two weeks in advance with the dates for broadcasting each greeting clearly listed and instructions to broadcast the greetings during the morning and afternoon registration times. The week before the event, a PowerPoint presentation (see Figure 5.4.1) of the greetings with embedded sound buttons was sent to each form tutor so that the students could read, listen and

Figure 5.4.1 Announcing the project in school

practise; this would also provide the opportunity to discuss different languages and in some cases, different alphabet and writing systems.

The project was a real success as indicated by students' enthusiastic engagement with it and the opportunity it provided for the school community to share what the headteacher referred to as 'our languages'. These were Arabic, Somali, Greek, Turkish, Romanian, Hungarian, Panjabi, Czech, Korean and Italian, and students and staff enjoyed hearing these languages integrated into the school day in a way that had not happened before.

6 A Conversation With Tawona Sitholé, Poet and Musician

1 Introduction

Tawona Sitholé, better known as Ganyamatope (his ancestral family name), uses his heritage to inspire him to make connections with other people through creativity, and the natural outlook to learn. Tawona worked on the Creating Welcoming Learning Environments project, outlined in Chapter 1, as a workshop leader, along with Alison Phipps (see Chapter 2, this volume). Tawona and Alison used activities with music and the spoken word to inspire teachers to integrate these techniques into their teaching. Tawona is widely published as a poet and playwright, and short story author. This chapter takes the form of a dialogue between Tawona Sitholé and Jane Andrews which explores Tawona's own artistic practices and his work as a teacher and facilitator working in a variety of educational settings and with learners of different ages.

Jane

Could you tell us about what you are working on at the moment?

Tawona

We've got a new project which is the South-South Migration Hub (MIDEQ – Migration for Development and Equality, funded by UKRI GCRF, see https://www.mideq.org/en/) – Because migration scholars know that most of migration happens in the global south, between low- and middle-income countries, it's trying to look at what's going on, what is that reality like, what are its mechanisms, what is happening on the ground? Twelve countries are involved which are turned into six corridors because there is migration between those pairings in the 12, so we have Malaysia–Nepal, China–Ghana, South Africa–Ethiopia, Egypt–Jordan, China–Ivory Coast and Burkina Faso, and Haiti–Brazil. So, we have corridor teams and work packages; in our work package, we are looking at creative arts and resistance and well-being. It's quite interesting because our previous work in the RM borders project is really coming to the fore in this project – we're finding that our emphasis on language is so important because that seems to have skipped a lot of our colleagues, the language component – when we shared the work we've done before people are finding it fresh and that's interesting in the conversation.

Jane

Are the creative arts in all of the work packages, and how many creative artists like you are there in this project?

Tawona

It is the four of us – Alison Phipps, Gameli Tordzro, Naa Densua Tordzro and myself, so what has happened is we are going to collaborate across the project, which is a challenge in itself. There is going to be a survey. It's been a difficult negotiation to get our two questions onto the survey. We want to ask two creative arts questions, but the census team were asking why do we want to know what artefacts or objects people carry with them, and how this helps in understanding migration?

Jane

That's a beautiful question! I'm glad you're asking that!

Tawona

Also we want to ask what idioms or sayings do people have relating to their home countries or travel itself or being in the destination countries?

Jane

I know you and Alison have talked about the concept of 'interruption' in terms of injecting new, creative ways of conducting research.

Tawona

Yes, it continues Jane and to be honest with you, there are lots of people who are not familiar with the arts. I think those who are welcoming of it or inviting us into their own process, I think that's the way we have to work. Some people don't have the time to go into this exploration because they are busy, there are so many factors, and some people are just too unfamiliar with the arts.

Jane

I think there's something interesting there – as human beings, we're sometimes like that, aren't we? Something that's unfamiliar can be scary or challenging that there's another way of looking at the world.

Tawona

In my work, some other interesting things are going on – I'm also working for the national theatre, and I'm teaching two classes: The younger class is the 8 and 9 year olds, and the older class is the 18 to 25. So that is an exciting journey because I am bringing in my storytelling and oral tradition sides and that is an adventure in itself.

Jane

What's your approach to teaching these groups?

Tawona

I tend to want to do something creative because devising, as you know, is one of my favourite things because it brings more out, in the end, from people. So even that alone, even that aesthetic alone, Jane, of standing, not holding a sheaf of paper, I'm just standing with some kind of strange objects, holding, maybe, some soft balls to throw around. The young people themselves are getting a lot out of it as they're learning how to write, create stories and do more of the production. For example, at the beginning of term, we sit down and plan what we are going to do for the term, so we discuss it so I can prepare and bring, and they said, no, they don't want to work off a script, so they fed that back to me.

Jane

There's such a strong methodology there in your way of working.

Tawona

When we went to Nairobi for the inception of the MIDEQ project, I missed a class, but while I was away, I wrote postcards to each of my classes. For me, this was a normal thing. The other thing I did was to share stories – the students can then play the stories on their own, they can find new endings to stories, and they can find their own versions of stories. Within those stories, we can introduce a character, then maybe at some point in the story, a group are travelling, and they are trying to see something precious, then while we are resting, we play a game – a game we played as kids in Zimbabwe. So you bring it into the context of the story – then, it's easier for the kids to remember the game – they know they played it in the story.

Jane

That's really lovely – it sounds to me that the seeds that you leave are like embedding practices in a way and allowing them to have an experience which can generate new practices.

Tawona

I like the way you've put it – yes, similar to the work we did in Bristol together – the idea of setting the ritual of the space – you're not just tumbling in and haphazardly doing things. For example, one little ritual I do with them is inviting the story into the space – some kind of chanting that invites the story in. We decide amongst ourselves 'what is our own ritual that we can make up?' And they are excited, so they start bringing all manner of physical things – maybe it's an action – in one of the classes, we had an invisible kind of lasso, and I'd say 'which corner of the room is the story coming in from?' And they'd argue about it and then with all of us are in some kind of tug of war set up, we'd pull the story into the room together. By the time we've finished doing all that, everyone is in the space, and you know they are really in the space, so it's amazing what happens. Also, we celebrate people's names – we do call and response to celebrate everyone's presence.

Jane

That's really lovely, thank you. I wanted to go back to idea about the drums. You've told me before that you took your drums in and the children in the school said, 'we've got some of those', but they went to a cupboard to get them out. It sounds as though they weren't routinely used perhaps?

Tawona

No, the drums weren't getting used, the kids actually said 'ah! You know, we do have drums here even though we don't use them' but that was the moment that unlocked those drums from their imaginations.

Jane

In my mind I have an image of the children using the drums more now that you have been there.

Tawona

Yes, I really hope so with the names – everyone drums their own name into the drum and the whole class responds back. For example, I go 'Ta-wo-na' 'ta-da-da' and then it's Jane – it's one syllable – Jane – ta – and everyone goes Jane – back.

Jane

It's beautifully simple, but it's personalised and also low on resource. I think sometimes in education we say 'oh if only we had more resources' but maybe we don't spend enough time thinking what we have got and how we can bring it into our daily practices.

Tawona

Also that is accompanied by me saying to begin there's no right or wrong way – I know we say it a lot but it's important to say it – the difference between a noise and a sound. Who decides? It's important to be inclusive of everyone's voice so that all can participate, quieter voices can be amplified and get a chance.

Jane

Can you tell me more about how you use stories in your teaching?

Tawona

There are different types of stories in the repertoire – you've got the 'how things came to be' type of stories. Why do the chickens walk around scratching on the ground? Because in that story the chicken borrowed a magic chiringiso (in the Ndau language) which is a mirror from the falcon because the falcon always looked immaculate the chicken was envious. The chicken decided to say to falcon 'how do you manage this look?' 'oh it's my secret mirror, I've got this magic mirror that I look into, and it shows me all angles of my body, my feathers and my back', and the chicken says 'you know, what I'd really like is to borrow this mirror', and the falcon says 'no way no way, you can't borrow the mirror', and chicken insists you know and they're good friends and eventually falcon relents, and he hands the mirror over, and of course you know what happens in drama, the mirror gets lost, so when falcon comes to claim the mirror, chicken doesn't have it and falcon gets angrier and angrier and eventually falcon decides that every time they return without the mirror being present they will take one of the chicks so that is why we see chickens walking round scratching the dirt furiously – they are trying to find the mirror!

Jane

That's a tragic story! Endlessly looking for something they're never going to find!

Tawona

Yes, and then there is the open-ended story where you have to make a collective decision. I used one of these recently as well in one of the classes. It was the year of drought, and food was scarce and one person amongst us managed to find a food source, but they hid it from the community. In the class, we were all dressed up in our fabric as we were the villagers. We've done our farming, we are sitting, resting, so one of us found this food source, so they were hiding it from everybody. They were sneaking off, and they were making all these excuses. It's funny as we know it's a folk tale, but when you bring it to the modern day, it's interesting what the children say – 'oh they're pretending they're going to the gym'! And 'they're talking on their phone'.

Jane

I love that – the old and the new together!

Tawona

Yes, the story continues, the person there is going for a walk in the park and in the end they get rumbled. At the point of them being rumbled, the story ends because we need to sit as a community and decide. Then you start to see the different characters in the room because some want to bring punishments. This story asks for us to use debating skills and children can learn about different aspects of society and the world these stories sit in. This is a dynamic, mutating process of storytelling, where we all tell the story together.

Jane

Can you explain your practices working with groups?

Tawona

When I meet the group, I avoid telling them about all my qualifications, that comes with time. It's very important when I meet a group of young people I share that story of why I love what I do.

Jane

Where does this come from, for you?

Tawona

It's from the living archive. I have a notepad close because little anecdotes drop in with my mum. I'm doing it this way because she says things in the moment in a natural way, for example, I'll be talking to her and she'll say, oh you know it's gonna rain soon – and I say why do you say that and she says oh didn't you hear that 'kwo-vir-a kwo-vir-a inenge yaa kuti tsvo tsvo tsvo' so she does that because there's a bird called kwovira, when the rain is about to come, they gather themselves these birds so they prepare for the rain coming so when they do that call they are gathering themselves the kwovira are just out of the window and the kwovira has been turned into words – kwovira kwovira before the sun goes down the rain will be pouring so that's the kwo-vira, inenge yaa kuti tsvo tsvo tsvo

Jane

That's lovely, so beautiful.

Tawona

Mum was saying to me recently you know we are in a way we are never complete sculptures – there are always artisans or artists working away chipping away at us.

It's an incredible image that she gave me because I recognised it even in this conversation we're in now that there is this continual art making, sculpture, making process – it's going on.

Jane

Your conversations with your mum sound lovely.

Tawona

They're getting even sharper now – I'm going ok! Hold on hold on! I'm writing them down, I tried to do it very discreetly before, but now she knows I'm writing things down and we just laugh about it – so anyway meeting the new group I think it's important for me – that aspect of it, even the person who is in the drama room for the first time can have access to that energy. The fact that I have nearly 20 years' experience in this work does not separate me from the young person who is also just about to go on a creative adventure. So, if I can say how much I love stories and relate to them my grandmothers telling stories and me loving reading and all those things of mine, I think there's something for the young people to connect with. That would be very different if I walked in and described my experience and all the works I've written and starred in and performed in. That would be a different introduction I think.

Jane

That's interesting. By doing that it sounds like you're positioning yourself as a participant, in the space.

Tawona

Thank you, Jane, I will describe it like that in future. When we started my very first term there we came in and we, the staff, were asked what the term ahead had in store for us. My one line was – 'this term was for us to know each other as a group'– that was all I wrote.

Jane

That's really interesting, so we have different ways of conceptualising what we are doing don't we when we work in a creative way. Can you talk more about what works well when you go into a school?

Tawona

I think the arts are certainly getting a bit more respect, and I think in terms of the literacy side, the creative writing side, there is some excitement from when you go into a school and you go into a classroom that there's already really exciting things going on. You can feel it. I think the welcome I get depends on the class and the culture of the classroom. The more welcomed I am, the more I realise they are excited to have a writer come in. The very last session I went to, all the staff rescheduled things to be in my class. They were very excited, and the young people could see clearly that everyone was excited to have a poet in the school. It's the way you know you're going to have a good session or project. You know right away that it's going to go well. There was the most beautiful energy – teachers joining in and being excited and doing all the tasks we're asking them. The idea of collaboration is key here; there's a recognition of the arts as not a bit of play but as something that you can continue. Many teachers recognise that if they approach literacy in a different way, in a non-reading context that can spark off a different interest in language, because some young people may struggle with reading.

Jane

So, in your opinion what is the value of a poet coming into school?

Tawona

I concentrate more on the creative process – the dreaming of words and the re-evaluating of words. You know you hear these anecdotes about the first colonisers arriving in a village in Tanzania and seeing the locals playing those kind of board games with diamonds. You know all those anecdotes, and I feel words are like those diamonds. We use words everyday, but those words are precious. I'm not one to praise precious stones or metals or whatever, but I think playing or exploring with words – that is my power. I want to think about what is everyone's super power. So I feel like knowing my role within that space is important and so my role is to say to the young people, look language is something we use day to day but there's magic in there, there's beauty, an amazing super power in this so this is how you might get to that super power. Let's play around with it, and you start like this, you can exaggerate things, give yourself a bit of drama, and this is what can end up happening and watching that realisation. You said before when people realise that they can do fantastic things, I feel my role sits within that. For me, I identify that for myself as a practitioner, that is where the value of my work lies.

Jane

What role would you like to see for the arts in the future in educational settings – whether schools or colleges or informal settings?

Tawona

I just want to wind back a little bit. One thing I've noticed is that people are very target driven. You have to have accomplished so much for you to be satisfied of your competence. For example, in filming, you have to have done a feature, a documentary, a small piece of fiction, whatever the portfolio requires. In the busy-ness of trying to accomplish all the different parts of the whole, there is a sense of tunnelling in that happens, I feel. At the moment most of my creative writing workshops, the evening ones – I have students from universities, I have retirees, I have students from colleges – I would say that's a big kind of demographic. Someone will say you know what Tawona I am doing my master's in literature I've got all my stuff to read and I've got these essays to write, but I just wanted to come and actually find my own creative thread. So, I feel the space is congested with trying to accomplish what is required that sometimes there's not enough room for exploration of that young person's voice. So that's what I feel about the college and university experience of literature and language; it seems somewhat restrained by curricula and requirements for passing. From my experience in informal settings, there is perhaps a greater sense of freedom, and a lot of people find it exciting to do something creative especially when there's a performative aspect to it. My wish for the arts is – I guess there are two things here. Broadly I think they need recognition. I think the arts suffer from this kind of vagabond kind of persona that they seem to hold. There is the view of the arts as purely entertainment and in many areas of our lives they don't quite fit in. If you ask the average person there are so many notions around artists – one stereotype is of people who are anarchic. For example, in my home country, wider society's image of the artist is largely a very negative one, quite a few people see artists as people who wake up and maybe take substances and just think of crazy useless ideas to society. This is from personal experience. Fadzai Muchemwa from the art school in Harare has taken over the running of the school, and she's actually introduced a staggered payment scheme for the students who are suffering from financial hardship. A lot of the students there (close to 60%), there is a common recurring story within the students' experience there, and a lot of them have been either pushed out of home – neglected, abandoned because they are pursuing art. In Zimbabwe, there are so many factors – our parents in the time Rhodesia didn't have access to education and now transfer that onto these generations who are going to school automatically – some parents are saying why are you wasting your precious opportunity to go to school and why do you want to go and do art?

Jane

What, for you, Tawona, is the relationship between the arts and languages? How do they work together for you in your practice?

Tawona

I think the first thing I would say is that arts are a gateway to other languages. I've been laughing about this as I've been thinking about it. As kids we learned other languages through say music for example or movies. Our English learning journey for us – until pre-school age, we were of course immersed in talking with our family, but once you go to school that's when English becomes more established so up till that point a lot of it is songs and seeing things on TV and copying things you're seeing on TV.

Jane

That's interesting!

Tawona

I think there's something quite interesting about that. There's an effortless engagement with other languages through copying a song that you like or maybe it's a line from a film so there's something interesting about that kind of popular culture. For us, TV certainly played a big role, for our learning of English particularly as that's what we were watching, and I know a lot of French-speaking African people had a similar experience watching French films. I think also maybe almost a reverse of that is for me when I'm doing storytelling. So, in the relationship between the art of storytelling and languages – for the story to work, the participants need to immerse themselves into the spirit of the story. So, they have to speak the words. I have to speak the words in English for them to know what the story is. But the particular song in the story that transforms this character into – there's one of the stories where there's someone who turns himself into a crocodile, and they sing a little song 'jakachaka jakachaka pugu mukahwire'.

For that moment to be true and for this transformation where this person turns into a crocodile, you have to do the [pugu mukahwire], so you then invite the audience into that spirit of the story, and so there is a permission for them to become that part of the story, where they become the spirit of that moment. So, there is that constant invitation to step into another language and own it. You step into it to make it really work because the character's transformation relies on you, so you're not like a learner where you are developing some competency over time. You have to step in and just own it, so it's a very kind of – sharp invitation! You're not being given the steps or building blocks.

Jane

You've just got to do it in the moment. That makes sense.

Tawona

There is the arts themselves as a language which is quite exciting. The time we started thinking about this with Katja, Gameli and Naa Densua (from the RM@Borders Project) when we were in our hub, we decided that if we say that the arts are a language, so there are certain things we need to see coming along with that. So, basically, our task was, if the arts are a language, what do they communicate? How do they communicate it? And then the final thing we touched on was, well, if they are a language then we should use that language. It's fine for us to say the arts are a language, but we need to functionalise them in some way, so we need to actually say 'Ok if the arts are a language how will that operate in time?' When I go into the classroom of course, I'm using English to thread between the pieces, but the main language that is going on actually becomes the sound and the rhythms so that becomes the language. When you're playing the drums, it's important to learn the different zones on the drum, what sounds they make and then you start doing the call and response. So that becomes use of the arts as a language. We also have the objects, when you are devising, for example, you have an object and that object can turn into anything. So, we take it in turns to have an object, someone will put it on their head and it will become maybe a hat, someone will lie on it as a pillow, someone will drink out of it. So, this is an ongoing exploration.

Jane

Can you talk more about how you like to work with objects and base your devising around objects?

Tawona

A very good example of this is the calabash. When we were in Ghana, we had something like 18 languages in the room. We'd come in, and we'd notice that we were always pulling things back to ourselves because we were leading in English, and they were following us. Eventually, Alison (Phipps) decided let's try to do 'English last' and see how it would work. So, what we did is we brought the object in – the calabash – and the first at least 15 minutes or so would be non-verbal. The calabash would be there, and we'd just come into the room. Instead of each of us giving greetings such as how are you doing, the calabash was there, so someone would take it and perform with it and around it and reimagine it for us. They were communicating something, so it was their body language; it was what they suggested the object to mean. Someone, for instance, might just kneel in front of it and just stare deeply into it. It was a very intense, sombre moment. Then, someone would maybe move more flamboyantly around the room with it. So, that was quite stunning to see that happening in the room as a way of us announcing our presence in the space together and sharing a different kind of greeting to each other. The object is a vessel of communicating something that is witnessed by all, so it's like a dialogue. It's a suggestion that is witnessed by someone who is in the conversation with you. In Zimbabwe, when we did our project with Alison (the Strengthening Young Leaders project), we found the clay pot was a more popular vessel there so we used that. We met with our eight young people who we were going to work with for the project, and we didn't speak about our project we just bought this clay pot. We explained to these guys that we're here and we're working together and so we'll just put the pot in the middle. I just did one small thing with it as an instigation, and all of a sudden, everyone took it and started suggesting what they were thinking and feeling. People put their dreams, fears, hopes whatever, through this vessel. Someone engaged with the object, and we all became witnesses.

Jane

That reminds me of when I spent the day with you, Katja, Naa Densua and Gameli in your arts lab in Glasgow. I remember going into the room, and there was a table and chairs there and without thinking I made myself at home and got my notepad out and was comfortable on my chair. One of you then said, 'could you just stand up now as we're not really going to work like this – this isn't how we work'. I felt really surprised thinking how can we not work around the table? What shall I do with my notepad? It was a completely different way of thinking about working but you said just now about embodying the communication and valuing that and I have to say it was so revolutionary for me to think I could spend a day working when I wasn't sitting at a table and chair.

Tawona

You guys were amazing for us, honestly, and till now we return to that so often because one of the things that is an impediment is if people are not engaging. It's the same as when you are teaching – if the people you are with are not engaging or offering, then you know things can't really go anywhere. Then, there's a drag on the whole experience. So, I guess the arts in relation to language they offer different, other avenues. In terms of language learning or language exchange, I'll give an example of doing something around a language, my grandmothers, for example. The storytelling scenario, the classical one, is the homestead, the fire is there, we're all sitting around the fire, it's like the glow of the fire that's the magic, this is the standard, but there's also sitting down and shelling nuts. I remember this from my childhood. You've got big baskets full of these ground nuts or peanuts and you're shelling them so you're sitting. There's a choreography as you're shelling these nuts, you are throwing the shells over there and the nuts over here so everyone is in this choreography together. But that choreography is a baseline for a higher level of interaction that's happening where a story, a very intense story, is being told, the body then becomes just so synched into what it's doing it just frees the soul or the mind so that it just deals with the story. So, there's that side of it as well – I don't know what that's called because it's almost as if the body is making way for the mind to really grab this story. So, yeah, I guess that is like the opposite of the example I gave before, but it is also quite an interesting situation.

Jane

> When you're talking about shelling the nuts, how freeing that is, I think that it's the routine rhythm because you don't need to think about it. With the storytelling around the fire sounds you're in a state of readiness maybe. I had a question about the way you all worked with dance in the RM@borders project. Do you want to say any more about that?

Tawona

> In preparation for the Ghana work, we did a retreat at Allanton Peace Centre (in Scotland) with the young people and at that retreat one of our young people had serious problems with reading text. So when that came out, as I'd scripted a short script to perform, so when we got to the script we kept running into this. It was a case of quickly noticing it and going ok 'everybody scripts down' and thinking on your feet and going in a different direction. That raised some important questions at that time. So, we needed to think – when this happens what do we do? So that was in the background. We were leaning more towards devising, so when we got to Ghana and we saw that we had these many languages that again became a problem. How do you write the multilingual script that apportions everybody fair representation? Which language comes with which? So, all those questions came up. Then, when you are in the room with young people, even when they come off the stage they don't just walk down the stairs, some will do a somersault and some will do some sort of fancy dance or whatever. It's the way they even stand up or sit down. So, I'm watching all this and thinking there's a language going on here. The way these young people are expressing themselves and the fact that we were in a dance context was very much present. Just the way that someone will lift something up or they will move from one room to another or someone will say pass me this thing. Just how they will do it. It's just so much in them that we just thought 'wow let's see what this makes'. So, then we started (with Alison), we pooled the themes we just started say in groups of four and five: 'Guys, in five minutes, can you show us a border, with no words' or 'Show us loneliness', 'Show us home sickness', 'Show us fear', 'Show us conflict'. Sometimes they would just do body shapes, sometimes action, and it just started making sense. There was so much in that vocabulary of movement that was so rich, and we then realised that wow there is so much to work with here. As you know, I'm a word-based practitioner, so this was a big thing for me. Of course, I use my body too but for me everything relies on the text I create to turn into spoken word. I think in the whole show (it's an hour and twenty minutes) it's only two or three parts during that whole time that there's any spoken word at all. And it's very brief, there's a refrain that happens in one of the scenes and then there's one scene when someone goes [jeen'e] which is one word, one phrase, then there's another few lines of poetry near the end. That's about it really, only those three parts but then the story is compelling, it's there it's comprehensive, with no dialogue. So that was exciting.

Jane

> It's so nice to hear you tell that as I hadn't heard that before as the work in Allanton working without a script is like the prologue to the work in Ghana. You were responding to one of the young people's preferences or difficulties and that led into this way of working in Ghana.

Tawona

This is the thing about relationships as well because Ignite (the theatre company we worked with in Allanton) – I've worked for the company for a long time now are so very dear to me, and these young people are very familiar to me – it was just such a moment that really sparked something because up till that point the young chap who this came up with I hadn't thought that about him before because he's otherwise very confident. So, sitting there and having made the presumption 'here's a script, pass it round and let's read'. Because that seems like a straightforward thing and then something happened. You think 'this isn't as straightforward as it looks' but then other avenues are possible.

Jane

And then that opened things up in Ghana. Thinking about the relationships, you were being really attentive to what the young people were communicating with you and then you were building on that.

Tawona

Yes, in Ghana, one of the biggest revelations was when we started using the calabash the dynamic changed. A lot of the young people are quiet, you go into the room and of course there's going to be the ones who are confident, as in any group, who will offer responses to things. Using the calabash we found, all of a sudden, we took notice of someone else and 'oh wow, that's very creative'. So, you start noticing different people because if you're working with the spoken word, the ones who are more confident, who always speak out, will always be visible but this was a different kind of atmosphere where you can notice 'ah ok we are seeing some characters who we don't normally notice at other times'. That was one interesting thing and then even further when we started using 'English last', we discovered two young people who were brilliant at translating, but in general, they were very quiet. When we first tried that out, we just asked that translation sequence to happen it would bring six to seven different routes before we got to English, but a couple of young people, two young women, stood out who really took that on. They were generally very quiet otherwise, but then they just put that across and when we were listening people would giggle, people would laugh. The response in the room was big whenever they started speaking and so we knew that there was something going on here and then we nurtured that as well. Those two young women, Mary and Ruth, they are brilliant at translating and that was one other thing that emerged from that. Also the conversation around 'is that the right wording?' when someone's translating and then others go 'ah no I think it's this', it creates a lot of dialogue as well, so it really became quite exciting, and we'd have had none of that if it wasn't for this young guy in Scotland who made us move away from the script and then getting to the ideas and using the calabash and so those decisions allowed us to go on that journey.

Jane

There are so many interesting things you've mentioned there Tawona. It's really interesting as you've pointed out you're a word-based practitioner and so it's totally reconceptualising what's going on with practice which without thought could be totally based only around words and scripts and languages in conventional ways.

You talked about your two translation experts, and it was almost as though you've repositioned languages in your practice because you allowed them in, but they were only allowed their creative space in the way that the calabash had its creative space and the dance moves themselves had their communicative space. So the translation work didn't come in at the top, above everything else, which is what can happen can't it?

Tawona

It was a discovery, yes.

Jane

Do you want to share with me what inspires you in your music and poetry and in your life?

Tawona

A few things! I think the best way to answer that is to give context for my inheriting the music and stories and if I can just talk about the people who I inherited those things from. In terms of the family, we have now the mbira which I play which is now the sixth generation of that instrument being passed down so it's got that distance that it's come. The stories are the same, it's passed down, passed down, passed down and shared, and we've lived the stories. It's quite interesting, Jane; I often call my mum up and say 'Mum! that story about the hare and the baboon, I only know it to half way how does it end again!' – I've got lots of fragments like that. It's a great story but how does it begin? I know that later on this happens…

If you think about the lives of those people, how they were living socially… it was Rhodesia, it was at that time what they called the 'colour bar', which was everything split by racial lines, quite a different experience. My own father grew up working on a plantation, a tea plantation, and my mother as a maid, that kind of thing, so within all that experience of being poor, hardship, enduring, whatever we want to call it, within that whole experience, all of those people taking that into consideration, you know how their social life was, what the difficulties were they went through, there's nothing that made them happier than when they were in that moment, when they were playing music, when they were telling stories. It was when they were most alive in that time, so it's to do with what they passed on intentionally and what I learned by observation. So I guess there's a thing about teaching and learning there, so of course our elders are always kind of giving us teachings, but there's also the learning by observation. They may not be aware that they are teaching at that time just observing how they are, how they are alive with it, so this is a massive thing for me because when I look at it, the history of that colonial experience is very harsh and very brutal in many ways but the arts, somehow, from the many journeys that were made before, I'm sure that there have been many difficulties in the past, but my most recent one that I'm aware of is this colonial period and so the fact that these arts are travelling through all these time zones, these political zones, these social zones and still continuing in their same life, giving reality is something that is very, very big for me. So that is a massive thing, so for me, it's the love of what the arts facilitate, in terms of socially, spiritually, whatever. The coming together and having a space where we can be open to each other, it's a massive thing, a massive thing. I would say if you want to distil what this means to me, this is it really. When I am going to perform or do something, I am so excited at the idea that there will be other people and I'm preparing myself and I want to do the best performance I can, whatever that is. I guess I'm fortunate in terms of nerves, but I'm so preoccupied by how exciting this moment is getting together, there's something quite special about a gathering. In the traditional gatherings, it was a community where people knew each other mostly who gathered together and they played and had their meal and people celebrated their life in five circles in the context of our socialising tradition. There's a circle, chisero, where people have a meal, then after the meal there's kuseredzera when we are just having light conversation, then there's the dariro which is kind of the performance circle, so people play songs, recite poetry, then you come to dandaro which is where everyone's resting after the high energy of dariro you pick up all the conversations: 'oh hi, how is work?' and then this is now the time to say 'so by the way, I didn't tell you that I'm having some difficulties – A-B-C-D' because when the conversation is a bit more light and everyone's meeting each other, you're not going to say 'Hello I've got a kidney stone!'

Jane

I see, you don't jump straight in with the big news!

Tawona

And the fifth circle is called the dare, and it's more like a council, a ritualised conversation where if you're dealing with important matters – your family or whatever scale you are working at. So for me now, when I go into a public space, people come from all over the place – I don't even know where they've come from, I don't know what their likes, dislikes or anything about them, but I have to engage in a meaningful way with them so that's quite exciting I think for me the underlying, the value in everything that I'm doing is just getting together and being open to each other the possibilities of what that brings. Because everyone brings so much into that space and we all come out enriched through that interaction but we come in, we make something, I often describe it as a bit like in chemical reactions. Sometimes you have to use a catalyst, and the only difference is that a catalyst comes out of the other side of the equation completely unchanged, unaffected by the process. I may be the catalyst because I'm the facilitator of this space, but unlike an enzyme I come out transformed also.

Jane

That's really beautifully expressed. I was thinking I can understand why you shouldn't feel nervous because your conceptualisation of the event isn't as a performance, of you putting something on, but it is like a natural sharing. If it's about relationships it isn't something to be nervous about is it it's about the possibilities – so we shouldn't be nervous about possibilities we should be ready for them and open to them shouldn't we.

Tawona

I like this – you've just explained something very important to me – yes, yes, 100% yes.

Jane

> *The five circles are almost like a grammar of being together. There is something that is right to say or do at a certain time..... This is the final question now – What do you hope the arts and different languages can offer to children and young people and adults in their lives?*

Tawona

> I'll respond first with what the arts have offered me. The arts have offered me an understanding that I wouldn't have had if I – you know everything in my lifestyle in Harare being an urbanite I had no window or any appreciation of what my grandparents' experience or knowledge was worth. I had no window whatsoever because in Harare living in the suburbs life was great, you know, according to what we thought. Parents working to keep things going and so we thought yes we are progressive, we are going to these desirable schools, so we thought we had the cutting edge of life and experience and of course we thought all knowledge was coming from the school teachers. But then having access to my grandparents (which my parents made sure in school holidays) I was always out there in an unlikely learning situation because you sit there and you think, you know it all, and then well wow what's going on here? Even if you look at a very basic thing like numeracy, for example, there's a skill these grandparents have. They have livestock, in Zimbabwe, cattle is the big thing, they have loads of cattle, they have goats, they have their granaries because if you look at their homes, they are built raised off the ground and then the floor comes, so granaries are built like that for aeration and to prevent submersion in water and those granaries, the stocks in there were kept for at least a year, a supply of food in case the rains don't come. So, if even one of the little calves went missing, my grandfather would know that even though there were many, close to a hundred in the homestead. So, this started showing little clues – it's actually a system, it's not the one I'm familiar with, but there's a serious system here that is effective and sustaining. So just observing that and going into the granary with my gran and she'd go 'oh yeah', you know elderly people they're not as physically able, and also the space is too small for an adult, so they send you into the granary, 'you go in and get this thing for me', and I lift this one, and she says 'no no no don't touch that that's for next year'. Wow! So, it's those small moments that you say 'wow ok' and of course the stories bring anecdotes and proverbs and idioms, so that richness of language. I was thinking of myself and the books I loved reading because I thought these things were unique to the books I was reading, but when I come to the stories again something is really real, so I think it allowed me to open up my experience to – somehow I wouldn't say that my society was doing that deliberately but – I'm not saying it was being done maliciously, but I was being closed down into one tunnel. The attitude of urban people in Zimbabwe, of Harare people is they look down on so-called uneducated rural people. So, I was one of those people just by default, but yeah a whole world was waiting there which is quite incredible, and I was fortunate, I was one of the few fortunate people who got to burst that mind barrier and this crazy world where art is there and there's just so much. So, I think the big lesson to that is being open– any moment can be a moment of learning, any encounter, any person you meet is a potential teacher. Someone who you meet in passing might give you some words or can impact your life in a major way cos I used to observe my mum out in Zimbabwe – my mum at the market, the vendors but that interaction, it was how my

mum spoke – the greeting, the poetic greeting of respect and what comes back in return – that is an amazing lesson for me in terms of learning, education, the fact that anybody has the potential to change a life. Anybody has the potential to teach you something profound, so I try to be open to that, and it can happen in the most unlikely circumstances and from people you least expect. So, it's a big learning experience for me so that's my personal one but in terms of what the arts can offer to young people and children, it's just the idea we spoke about before about the different ways of doing things, the different ways of expressing ourselves. I guess just now in my current work in Zimbabwe, I'm very much fighting against what pop culture is doing, young people have set their sights on flashy things – all their heroes are the people who drive flashy cars, and I try to say there's also something cool about making a piece of art, there's something cool about being able to express yourself in other ways, in being someone who can see something in the neighbourhood and say guys why don't we intervene – what about this idea – it comes from the centre of the individual. But the community is more at the centre of our experience as we have an idiom that says the unit is the society rather than the individual, it's that whole idea – kuwanda huuya.

6.1 Creative Arts Processes for Working With EAL Children

Anna Comfort
St Michael's on the Mount Primary School, Bristol, UK

'The Magic Shoes' Project

As an experienced primary classroom teacher in Bristol inner-city schools, I have come to fully understand the challenges that come with integrating new arrival non-English speakers into both a school and classroom environment.

I have been teaching at St Michael's on the Mount Primary School in the heart of Bristol for more than eight years. St Michael's can have more than 27 different spoken languages at any one time. It is a transient community. Many children's parents are studying at the university for as little as one year at a time. There is often little, if any, extra support given to these children. Teaching assistants usually only work one-to-one with SEN children. While working as the EAL coordinator, I have continued to discover that using singing and drama is a particularly effective and enjoyable way for EAL students to learn English.

The Magic Shoes project, named after our first musical, is very much part of my school's ethos – to celebrate the cultural diversity of our learners. It provides them with an opportunity to perform to the whole school and really embraces their progress and development in learning English as a new language.

'The Magic Shoes' and the more recent play 'The Magic Hat' are two musicals which I asked Catherine Matthews, a playwright who has worked with EAL students, to write. The songs were adapted and produced by a professional musician, Richard Lobb.

The first play, 'The Magic Shoes', is about a lonely boy called Hari who finds some magic shoes which take him to the moon for an adventure. On the moon, he makes friends with a Moonie called Dop, and they briefly return to Earth together. It explores the themes of communication, sense of belonging and friendship, all of which are very relevant to children who have left their homes, families and friends to move to a new country. The second play, 'The Magic Hat', is about a brother and sister called Peter and Maya who have to make a journey across a forest to find their parents. Their grandmother gives them a magic hat which allows them to communicate with the creatures of the forest. This play explores similar themes to the first.

The project runs for 12 weeks and is led by a project leader and a musician. I have developed work schemes and resources, which include the week's objectives, activities and language focus (see examples at the end of this chapter). The language focuses are tied to both the story of the play and the vocabulary needed for the script. They are also closely linked to the National Curriculum in England.

Larger parts are given to more fluent speakers, but there are enough parts (20–25) for all levels. EAL learners are selected from the different year groups by their class teacher and, in the past, some have been put forward by other schools. They are selected on the basis of need. Usually, this would mean that newer students with less English are selected. Previously, children from these countries have participated: Somalia, Algeria, Turkey, Spain, Brazil, Iraq and Syria.

The main focus of the project is to develop children's confidence in speaking English in small groups, whole class and eventually whole school contexts. Taking risks and 'having a go' is key to learning a new language. Using drama and music encourages students to grow and gain in confidence and enables them to take those risks.

The project helps provide them with sound building blocks on which to continue developing their language skills with more confidence and accuracy. Constant repetition through learning lines and songs, and hearing and re-hearing the rhythms of common phrases in the English language are enormously helpful in embedding a new language. Over the past five years of the project, I have noticed how much the children's speaking and listening skills have improved.

The project also brings social benefits. It has enabled the children to build friendships with other children across the school who share similar language barriers. Parents are invited to each session to help make scenery and costumes. It has been a very effective way of helping new parents become more involved in their children's school life. It also provides them with an opportunity to meet other parents who may have little or no English and who have only recently arrived in Bristol. The remaining pages of this chapter give examples of our practice to bring the project to life for you. They show you three weeks of work schemes showing session objectives and classroom activities along with examples of drama games.

Work scheme – Week 1
Where do we want to go?

Session objectives

The emphasis of this session should be on raising multilingual awareness through song, play and experimentation, and allowing your multilingual students to draw on their own language resources to help them with learning English. Children will be learning to:

- Introduce themselves and get to know each other
- Think about different countries around the world and to say hello in each other's languages
- Use their voices expressively and creatively when singing songs and speaking solo lines.

Language focus

- Use the sentence start *'I want to go to...'*
- Understand and respond to the questions: 'Where do we come from?' and 'Where do we want to go?'

Resources

- Ball (preferably a globe ball) to pass round the circle
- 'Hello' game*
- Flashcards of key vocabulary*
- Flip chart to record children's ideas
- Strips of paper for solo lines
- Pictures of Hari and the Magic Shoes*

*in resource pack

Activities

Introduction:
Firstly, children sit in a circle. As they pass round, or roll, a globe ball, they introduce themselves. Model correct language, e.g. *'My name is ... I can speak...'*
Elicit from children what they all have in common (speakers of other languages).
Play the 'Hello' game – see Drama games.

The play:
Talk about the beginning of the story using character pictures for support.

Song 1:
Introduce the first song 'There are so many places to go'.
Focus on writing new lines for the song with their ideas, e.g. *'I want to go to... because...'*
Give lots of examples, e.g. *'I want to go to China to see where dragons live'; 'I want to go to India to sleep in my old bed'.*
The musician and project leader sing the chorus of the first song together and sing their own examples of where they would like to go to. The children then work with the musician and leader, and with any other adults present, to think about their own lines starting with *'I want to go to...'*. Write down all the ideas. Musician practises singing lines aloud with children. Groups then choose the best ideas and produce written verses so that each child (or pair of children) has a solo line to sing.

Plenary:
Whole group comes back together and sings first song all together. Choose more confident children to call out solo line.

Homework:
Each child takes their line, written on a strip of paper, home to practise.

Work scheme – Week 2
Will we get there soon?

Session objectives

Before this session think about how creating a multilingual space should be a joyful experience where the children can get used to unfamiliar sounds and acknowledge the language riches of all multilingual learners. Children will be learning to:

- Sing with confidence and in time
- Use spoken language to develop understanding through imagining and exploring ideas
- Listen and respond appropriately to adults and their own peers.

Language focus

- To use and respond to question *'Will we get there soon?'*
- Use sentence *'I hope we're nearly there now.'*
- To learn new vocabulary: *drama, journey, space, Earth, rocket, moon, planets, stars, flowers, home, drama.*

Resources

- Mini whiteboards
- Bustling market square game*
- Words for Song 1*
- Pictures of characters and story so far*
- Flashcards of key vocabulary*
- Space activity sheet*

Activities

Introduction:
Play the **'Bustling market square'** game.
Song 1: Start by all singing with new song sheet. Children sing their solo lines loudly and clearly. Repeat this as a group until confident.
The play:
The children listen and watch the telling of the story of 'The Magic Shoes' (until the Moon song) by the project leader and the musician. Create a mini stage, if possible, with gym mats. Sit the children in rows as an audience. Select some children to hold flashcards of main characters and to hold them up when they hear them in the story, e.g. the Moon, Hari, Magic Shoes. Musician to use pictures to tell the story and ask for volunteers to come to the front and hold pictures up when appropriate. Ask children questions after the performance about what they liked about the story. Tell them how the project leader and musician used their bodies and faces to show how the characters were feeling. Discuss the meaning of the word 'drama'. Talk about going on a journey. Ask the children if they've made a long journey before? Where did they go? What mode of transport did they use? How long did it take? Children share and discuss their stories in small groups. Ask children to think about going to the moon. What would you see in space? How would you feel? Teach new vocabulary using pictures, where needed, to support them with answering these questions and composing their own sentences.
Song 2:
Listen to the musician singing the beginning of Song 2. Ask children to identify the question in the song *'Will we get there soon?'* Practise saying this question as a group. Then split the group into two where the first group says *'I hope we're nearly there now'* and adds an appropriate action, and the second group says *'Will we get there soon?'* and also adds an appropriate action. Practise this in speaking form and then singing it as in the song.
Plenary:
Learn the rest of the song, stopping to show flashcards for new vocabulary, such as meteor and comet etc. Children think of more actions for this song.
Homework:
Children to practise both songs at home and complete Space activity sheet (in resource pack).

Work scheme – Week 3
Who are they?

Session objectives

This week's focus is on raising multilingual awareness by exposing the group to new language sounds and rhythms and reflecting on what hearing a language without understanding it really feels like. Children will be learning to:

- Understand that communication isn't only about language
- Ask relevant questions to extend their understanding and knowledge
- Sing solo and as a group, using their voices with increasing accuracy, fluency, control and expression.

Language focus

Identify and use question words with accuracy.

- **What** do they look like?
- **Where** do they come from?
- **How** do they live?
- **What** do they eat?

Resources

- Pictures of characters*
- Gibberish scenarios *
- Large picture of Moonies *
- Flashcards of question words *
- Question-asking activity *
- Percussion instruments

* in resource pack

Activities
Introduction:
Play Gibberish (see Drama games) with the whole group. The project leader, musician and another adult model it first and then choose three more confident children (or parents!) to have a go while the rest of the group has to guess what they are talking about. After this activity ask the questions:
- **What** does it feel like to not understand but still have to communicate?
- **What** other ways of communication did you have to use besides language?
- **How** did you work out what they were talking about?

Songs 1 and 2:
Sing Songs 1 and 2 as a whole group. Practise solo parts where necessary and clarify actions.

The play:
After recapping on last week's telling of the story, the leader continues the story and explains that Hari has now arrived on the moon with the Magic Shoes. Although, at first, he and the Magic Shoes think there is nothing there, they suddenly spot some strange creatures waddling towards them. Show pictures of the Moonies and encourage children to use question words to ask their own questions: 'Who are they?' and 'Where do they live?'. Musician to record children's questions as a mind map around a Moonie picture.

Song 3:
The musician teaches Song 3 about the Moonies. Introduce the new characters of the story. Develop an understanding of rhythm and explore how percussion instruments can be used in music for a range of purposes.

Plenary:
Sing all three songs together.

Homework:
Complete the question-asking activity from the resource pack.

Drama games

'Hello' game
This is an excellent way to welcome everyone and embrace the cultural diversity of the group. Children and adults stand in a circle all together. Take it in turns to go around the circle. Each child and adult says 'hello' in their home language and adds a gesture. For example, 'Shalom' could be followed by a bow; 'Bonjour' could be followed by blowing two kisses. After everyone has said 'hello' and made their gesture you go back to the beginning. After the first person says 'hello' and makes their gesture, each person repeats it one after the other until you reach the next person who is to share theirs. When you have completed the circle, you can then go around quicker and quicker to see how well you can remember them all.

The bustling market
This follows on from the 'Hello' game and can be shared over two sessions, so that everyone has a go. Remind everyone of how to say 'hello' in each person's language by forming a circle and saying 'hello' with the appropriate gesture. Explain that now they are going to pretend they are in a busy market square. They are going to go round the market square meeting new friends and greeting each other with a friendly 'hello' in different languages. Choose one child to stand on a chair, then explain how their job is to call out a country that someone in the group comes from, e.g. Germany. Everyone is to then walk around greeting different people with a 'Guten tag' and the gesture that went with it from the 'Hello' game. Every two minutes the child will shout out a new country, and the greeting and gesture changes accordingly.

Tongue twisters
Tongue twisters are great for helping kids concentrate on working all their articulation muscles. After practising them, get the group to stand in a circle, then ask each student to say the tongue twister using a different emotion (angry, sad, happy, scared, frustrated, confused, etc.) Or, beginning with the first student to your right, challenge them to begin happy but to gradually get more and more angry. Students take turns around the circle.
Examples:
'Toy boat. Toy boat. Toy boat.'
'The big beautiful blue balloon burst.'
'Flora's freshly fried fish.'
'Smelly shoes and socks shock sisters.'

Pantomime warm up
This helps with learning each person's name and something about them, as well as with understanding how to pantomime and communicate ideas. Gather students in a circle. Each student says their name and makes a gesture on each syllable. The action should be simple and can demonstrate an interest they have, or something they do every day, e.g. the name Pam-e-la and a paddle stroke on each side of their body – one stroke per syllable – to show they like to paddle a canoe. Each student says their name individually and demonstrates the gesture, then everyone repeats the name and gesture. Repeat the process around the circle until all have shared their name and gesture.

Drama games continued

Gibberish
Arrange everyone into groups of three. Give each group a mini dialogue in a different language that has three parts to read. Explain that they will not be able to understand them. Each group should decide who is person 1, 2 and 3. On the back of the gibberish sheet should be a clue to what the dialogue is about. This should give an indication of what emotions the three people should be showing, e.g., they are arguing over a football match, they are saying goodbye at an airport, or they are congratulating one another for passing their exams. The groups practise reading the dialogues for five minutes and then perform them to the whole group. The whole group has to guess what the dialogue is about, despite not understanding the actual words, through watching the readers' facial expressions, body language and the change in intonation in their voices showing their emotions. Afterwards have a discussion about language asking questions such as:

- **What** did it feel like to not understand but still have to communicate?'
- '**What** other ways of communication did you have to use besides language?'
- '**How** did you work out what they were talking about?'

The sun shines on
Arrange the class in a circle with one chair for each person and one person standing in the middle. The person in the middle uses the expression 'The sun shines on...' and completes the sentence, e.g. 'The sun shines on everyone who has a sister'. Everyone who this applies to has to get up and sit down in a different chair. The last person to sit down ends up in the middle of the circle. They then complete the sentence in a different way, e.g., 'The sun shines on everyone who ate pasta last night' and so on…

Welcome ice breaker
Stand or sit in a circle and go around the group with everyone saying their name and something they like which begins with the same letter: 'My name is Parminder and I like parachuting.' Reassure the group that in drama you are pretending so it doesn't have to be true.

Buzzy bees
Step One: On 'Go', your students move around the game space pretending to be bees, buzzing and flapping their tiny insect wings.
Step Two: After a short time of buzzy warm up, announce a letter, e.g. 'P'.
Step Three: Next, begin to count down from ten. During this time your students need to adopt the pose of something beginning with that letter. It can be a noun, verb, adjective, anything at all. For example, for the P letter you might be plump, pig, pleased, puffy, picky or pumpkin. On zero, your students must freeze on the spot.
Step Four: Now roam around the game space and ask each student in turn what they are. If two students say the same thing consecutively, they sit out the next round.

6.2 GCSE English, Using Poetry Written in Students' First Languages

Dominique Moore

For five years, I was Programme Leader, Bilingualism and English as an Additional Language (EAL) at a Bristol Secondary School. The school had a strong commitment to ensuring students maintained a good level of proficiency in their first languages as well as developing high levels of proficiency in English. The school taught GCSEs (school leaving examinations at age 16) in Arabic, French and Spanish with Urdu as an extra-curricular subject. The school offered Polish and Somali as Modern Foreign languages in KS 3 (ages 11 to 14) and facilitated early sitting of GCSEs in students' home languages. The school made use of the Languages Ladder[1] for the KS 3 Somali and Polish MFLs. The school ran an Institute of Linguists Level 2 translation qualification.

It was one of the most diverse schools in Bristol, 47% of students were Black, Asian and Minority Ethnic of which 43% were either bilingual or at various stages of learning EAL. This included British born bilingual students and students who arrived in KS 1, 2, 3 and 4 (from ages 5 to 16). Some of these students were asylum seekers, refugees and unaccompanied asylum seeking children. Some students had recently arrived to re-join parents who were refugees. Many of the asylum seeker, refugee and family reunion students had gaps in their education; some had no experience of formal education. There were also children of recent European migrants, most were Polish speakers. There were students recently arrived from the Indian subcontinent, the Philippines and the Middle East. These students usually had age-appropriate levels of education. The school received up to 30 new students a year as in-year admissions. There was significant student mobility, for example, asylum seekers being re-settled in other parts of the country once their status as refugees was confirmed. Some recently arrived students moved because of changes in their parents' employment.

The school provided an EAL option for KS 4 students. The lessons were for students most of whom had arrived in Year 9 or 10 (aged 14 and 15). The group included recently arrived students with age-appropriate education and students with limited or interrupted education who had arrived in Year 8 and continued to need additional support to fill gaps in subject knowledge and skills. The focus of the support in this

EAL option was on English as a GCSE subject. Most of the students in this option had also received additional EAL support in developing a command of English.

Most students had been encouraged to choose this option because, with additional support, it was believed they would have a chance of passing English GCSE in Year 11. Some students with very limited English and little or no experience of formal schooling were also part of the group. It was understood that they were unlikely to be able to achieve a pass at GCSE in Year 11 but could take the GCSE in Year 12 or later.

As part of the English GCSE curriculum, students were being asked to respond to and analyse poetry. Due to a limited command of English, many found the first step of the process, reading and developing an understanding of the poems, quite challenging, making the next step, analysing and responding to the poems, even more daunting. In order to develop the skills of responding to and analysing poetry, I decided to try to reduce the challenge of understanding the poems by finding work in students' first languages. In the lessons, with access to online translation and collaboration between students, we would develop the skills of responding to and analysing poetry. Response and analysis would take place in students' first languages and in English. The two biggest language groups in the classes were Polish and Somali. I decided to start with a Polish poem but made sure I informed the students we would also be repeating a similar activity in Somali and any other languages with appropriate poetry easily available in translation (there was no budget for resources for this GCSE option).

A Funeral

I searched for poems translated from Polish to English and found what I thought would be an easily accessible the poem 'A Funeral'[2] by the Nobel Prize-winning Polish poet Wislawa Szymborska. The lesson was their first after a one-week break, and I started the lesson by asking them to talk to each other about what they did during the break. I walked around taking some notes of parts of their conversation. I then asked if anyone was happy to share what their partner had told them. I also took some notes from what they said.

The class were then each provided a copy of the poem 'A Funeral' in English and in Polish but with the title removed. The students were asked to read the poem to themselves and asked to work out in pairs what they thought the poem might be about. Those still in the early stages of acquiring English who were not Polish speakers were in groups or pairs with more proficient speakers of English and also were encouraged to ask Polish speakers for help. I monitored the discussions and drew attention to particular lines and asked on what occasions people might speak about someone in this way. The students engaged well in the discussions.

Before they were asked to share with the whole class what they thought the poem was about, I asked the Polish-speaking students if anyone would be happy to read the poem aloud. Several volunteered; one was chosen and confidently read the poem aloud. The class were offered the opportunity to respond to hearing the poem in the language it was written.

I asked the students for feedback on their discussions. In this way, the class began to build an understanding of the poem. They recognised it as a series of conversations between pairs or groups of people; they came up with suggestions of possible situations where these conversations took place but did not suggest a funeral. I then gave the students the title of the poem and asked them to look at the poem again. The poem's title revealed the subject of the comments to the students. Students then responded orally to the poem now its subject was clear.

In order to look at the idea of how a poem might be written, I asked the students for some of the comments they had noted from their conversations at the start of the lesson, about what they had done during the break. These were written up on the board, and I added comments I had noted. I then asked the students to work in pairs or groups to try to make something that resembled a poem from the comments. I informed them that poems can come from real conversations, comments or incidents and that poets use these to explore ideas or express feelings. The students were told they could change lines, add new content, change the order of the comments and add whole lines. I briefly demonstrated how a comment could be added to and explained my thinking for changing that line. I selected another line and paired it with the new line, again explaining my thinking. The students then had a go at doing the same and shared their ideas, other students responding to each group's contributions. The lesson finished with brief biographical details about the poet.

I asked the students for some feedback on the lessons. The Polish speakers found the approach very helpful as they were very easily able to understand the poem, respond to it and more easily able to speak about the poem. Somali speakers and speakers of other languages were able to develop a better understanding of the poem collaboratively, including with help from Polish speakers.

The students said that using their transcribed comments from the conversations at the start of the lesson and then crafting these into something like a poem helped them understand how a poet might be inspired and how they might go about composing a poem. The process of collaboratively working on choosing the order in which statements were placed and also rewriting some comments to fit in the poem helped the students understand how a writer will draft, re-draft and craft a piece of work.

The Dusty Foot Philosopher K'naan

A similar approach was repeated with Somali. The search for a Somali poem available in translation and suitable for use in a lesson proved to be more challenging. There were Somali poems available online from The School of African and Oriental Studies, translated by Dr Martin Orwin https://www.soas.ac.uk/cts/translations/ but at the time those available were either quite lengthy or written for older audiences.

The Somali Canadian rapper K'naan had at the time released a CD entitled The Dusty Foot Philosopher. One of the tracks on the album includes lyrics in English and a refrain in Somali from a famous Somali poem. In the lesson, I played the track and was pleased to hear the Somali students joining in with the refrain; the poem was familiar to them. They explained they had heard it a lot at home. The other students in the class enjoyed the spontaneous participation of the Somali students. The evident appreciation of the Somali students helped to engage everyone in the lesson. The lyrics had been printed for all the class. The Somali students translated the refrain into English and explained the poem to the class. I shared some biographical information about K'naan including his leaving Somalia as a refugee. Some of the Somali students volunteered information about their similar journeys and feelings about having to leave their country. One of K'naan's aunts had been a famous Somali poet. I explained that one of the early British adventurers to visit Somalia had described it as the Land of Poets, poetry playing a very important role in Somali culture as it does in many parts of Africa. There was a short discussion on the differences and similarities between rap and poetry before exploring the lyrics in depth and students in pairs or groups responding to the poem, this time making some notes before sharing their responses with the whole class. There was a high level of student engagement; the Somali students expressed pleasure at hearing their language used in the classroom and having aspects of their culture and experiences explored in a lesson.

The use of students' first languages in lessons can have many benefits. It can allow students to gain an understanding of lesson content more rapidly and at greater depth. It helps engage those students at an earlier stage of learning English. It demonstrates a valuing of students' linguistic backgrounds. It allows students to maintain a level of proficiency in their first languages. The use of resources that positively reflect students' cultural backgrounds increases engagement of all students. Students from other cultural backgrounds benefit from learning more about each other. Both contribute to developing positive attitudes to cultural and linguistic diversity and help prepare students for life in a diverse society.

Notes

(1) The Languages Ladder; Steps to Success, Department for Children, Schools and Families, https://allconnectblog.files.wordpress.com/2015/01/ks2-progression-module-languages-ladder-dcsf-00811-2007.pdf
(2) A Funeral by Wislawa Szymborska, in Polish, https://polska-poezja.com/wislawa-szymborska/pogrzeb-4/ and translated from the Polish by Mikołaj Sekrecki, https://inwardboundpoetry.blogspot.com/2013/04/930-funeral-wislawa-szymborska.html

7 The Welcome Banner: Cultural Exchange Through Creative Collaboration

Luci Gorell Barnes

1 Introduction

In this chapter, I will describe the 'Welcome Banner', a participatory creative project that I facilitated with the Branching Out group at Speedwell Children's Centre in East Bristol. I will begin by describing the context and methodology of the work, followed by an account of making the banner itself and our reflections on it. Branching Out is part of East Bristol Children's Centres' offer to local families with young children and is attended by women, many of whom have English as an additional language (EAL). I will discuss how working in an inclusive way supports participants to develop a sense of personal agency and collective ownership of the group and examine why I think that this ethos is important in the light of postcolonial practice. I will try to reflect the cooperative nature of our work by including the voices of my colleagues and participants, beginning with Lindsey Fuller, headteacher at Speedwell, who describes the nature of the group.

2 Context

> The Branching Out group is run with a uniquely creative and inclusive approach. It is a universal group; participants do not need to be referred although many are signposted to the group as it is particulalrly good at meeting the needs of women from a diverse range of cultural and ethnic backgrounds, many of whom are new arrivals to this country. The creative approach breaks down cultural barriers as participants share their own lived experiences in many different parts of the world, through a range of artistic and environmental themes. Everybody is valued and their heritage cherished. Being part of the group has nurtutred participants' sense of belonging and wellbeing, increased their self-worth and confidence, and reduced social isolation.

I am a freelance socially engaged artist, and I have worked part time as Artist in Residence at Speedwell Nursery School and East Bristol Children's Centres (EBCC) since 2004. We work as a cluster of state maintained settings, and our reach area includes those ranked in the lowest 10% city wide in terms of overall deprivation[1] with 28.13% of our children currently on free school meals. At the time of writing, we have 96 children at the nursery and 24 of them have EAL.

I run an ongoing group called Branching Out, which takes place at Speedwell Children's Centre on Tuesday mornings in term time. It is designed to enable some of our more socially vulnerable parents to participate in creative group projects and is supported by a free crèche run by two workers in an adjacent room. The group is open by invitation from EBCC and Speedwell Nursery School staff, and some participants bring along friends who they think will benefit from it. As well as the crèche, the continuous provision includes myself as an experienced facilitating artist, free refreshments, access to art materials and books, information about health, money, housing, education and training opportunities, drug and alcohol issues, domestic violence and signposting to other services. Participants receive a WhatsApp reminder from me the day before the group, and this forum is also used as a place where we share photos and information relevant to the projects we are working on together.

The group aims to support people to build self-confidence, develop friendships and make positive social networks for themselves and their families, and I design art processes to facilitate these aims. I monitor and evaluate the group on a weekly basis to ensure that the benefits of it are robust and evidence based. We also have a group journal (see Figure 7.1) into which people are encouraged to paste photos taken during the sessions and to write their own observations in the language they feel most comfortable using.

While a few members of Branching Out are born and bred Bristolians, the majority have EAL. The group provides a space where people can practice speaking and writing English, and they are encouraged to help each other with translating and

Figure 7.1 Branching Out's group journal. Photograph by Luci Gorell Barnes

scribing when needed. If someone has EAL, it may mean that they are quite newly arrived here and have other specific issues that need tending to. Some of our EAL families have come to the UK to work or study, while many others are here as refugees or seeking asylum. Many of the women who come to Branching Out are from Somalia, Eritrea, Nigeria, Sudan and Kurdistan, and it would be disingenuous not to acknowledge the enormous impact of UK foreign policy on the outcomes of these and other countries. We also need to be conscious of the Islamophobia and racism that many of our families are subjected to on a daily basis, and the difficulties that they have experienced reaching the UK and then gaining asylum once they are here. In Branching Out, I try to create an ethos where we wonder what assistance and awareness people might need. Maybe they could do with a warm welcome and some extra support to develop their sense of belonging here? Maybe the culture they have come from is quite different and needs to be respected and reflected in their new environment? Maybe they have been through traumatic situations that have increased their feelings of vulnerability? Maybe they are juggling how to integrate into UK society without losing their own sense of identity? In the interest of building happy and healthy communities, I think it is important that there are spaces where these issues can be addressed, and schools and Children's Centres seem to be obvious places to make this kind of friendly contact.

3 Process

By engaging in an art project, participants can create something specific to themselves that then exists in the outside world, and making the outside world align more closely with one's internal landscape can have a powerful and often therapeutic effect. In addition, contributing one's individual expression to a shared artwork can increase people's sense of belonging and connection to each other. For a participatory art process to be effective in building participants' confidence and connectedness, it is crucial that they feel safe to express themselves freely and try out new ideas. Matarasso (2019: 75) argues that because of its ambiguous and oblique nature, the art process is 'a protected space in which to express identity, beliefs and experience'. While I agree with this idea in principle, I think that for the space to really feel 'protected' for *all* participants, it is crucial to consider issues of access and to work gently and responsively to enable those with marginalised voices to come forward and feel heard.

Considering these thoughts, I find Mary Watkins' discussion of the 'decolonization of "helping" professionals' (among which I number) very useful in framing my practice. She writes about developing conversational ways of working alongside others that

> ... build mutual respect and understanding, to create effective solidarity, and to contribute to the empowerment of those who have been marginalized. (Watkins, 2019: 19)

On a practical level, this means that I invite participants to suggest their own ideas for creative projects. I think of our projects as (often visual) anthologies inasmuch as they contain individual contributions that speak to a common theme. I try to follow the interests and concerns of the group and design creative collaborations in which people can share diverse views and experiences in ways that foster respect and understanding. This design element is crucial because it ensures that people's individual pieces are made with a view to the whole, and this approach allows separate elements to echo and resonate with each other within a congruent artwork. By working in this collaborative, mosaic form, participants can choose the level of participation that suits them best, while the overall design of the piece guarantees that their contribution will sit harmoniously in among others.

I occupy a dominant position in the group as a result of my skill and confidence levels as a professional artist, as well as holding the overview of the projects we engage in. Matarasso suggests that artists use their authority in ways that are both positive and negative for participants and reminds us that:

> Good intentions can mask but not justify actions that effectively subordinate people to the wishes of those with power. (Matarasso, 2019: 107)

Consequently, I try not to make assumptions about other cultures and freely acknowledge that I learn much more from my group than I will ever teach. I resonate with Leeson who stresses how important it is for people to characterise their unique perspectives, safe in the knowledge that these are welcomed and cherished. She writes:

> If people are to work across difference, they therefore need to feel that their own identities, whether individual or group, are valued and free to be defined by themselves. (Leeson, 2018: 104)

With this in mind, I invite celebrations of our diverse cultures in a number of different ways. These include encouraging people to bring food from home to share and to taste the food of others; making Ramadan calendars for the nursery children; celebrating Eid with mehndi and handmade decorations; and baking gingerbread and weaving midwinter wreaths from willow and ivy.

I try to wear my leadership role as lightly as possible by endorsing peer teaching and learning, and I rarely demonstrate something if there is a participant present who could teach it instead of me. Where appropriate I contribute to the projects myself, and sometimes I present other pieces of my artwork to the group to show that I value subtle and tacit experiences, perspectives and ideas. I try to allow myself to be seen as vulnerable by sharing aspects of my memories and background, and contributing some of my own experiences – with parenting for example – to group conversations. I understand my role as being to set the tone of the group and the creative ethos in which we are working. I always aim to hold people in what Rogers (1951) refers to as 'unconditional positive regard' inasmuch as I try not to make negative judgements about what people are creating or bringing to the sessions. I observe that my participants know their concerns and are working towards their own solutions, so my role is to facilitate reflexive processes in order to support the positive changes that they wish to make.

I have observed that engaging with creative practice gives people the chance to hear their own voice, as well as the voices of others, and I think that Branching Out can be understood as an ongoing action research project, in which any given inquiry:

> ...both emerges from and contributes to a complex and panoramic view of the world in which one lives and one's own particular place within it. (Wicks *et al.*, 2008: 17)

The sculptor Doris Salcedo suggests that 'art sustains the possibility of an encounter between people who come from quite distinct realities', and to this end, I offer creative processes to facilitate the expression of individual perspectives as part of a shared purpose. Respect, openness and warmth are key elements in this approach, and as Freire writes:

> Love is at the same time the foundation of dialogue and dialogue itself. (Freire, 1972: 89)

In this way, Branching Out is not just an art group; rather, it works as a facilitated space where participants can talk about things that matter to them. My participatory practice is not so much about the artworks that get made (although wonderful things are created, and they are not unimportant), but more about the interactions that happen during the creative process. Our discussions cover subjects that include child rearing, money issues, work and education choices, food, ethnicity and the practice of Islam and other religions. As Mary Brydon-Miller points out:

> A key value shared by action researchers, then, is this abiding respect for people's knowledge and for their ability to understand and address the issues confronting them and their communities. (Brydon-Miller *et al.*, 2003: 14)

By collaborating creatively in a forum where people's ideas and experiences are valued, we have found that meaningful social connections are made, and people develop a sense of agency, often becoming dynamic social actors in their communities.

4 Making the Welcome Banner

One example of our shared creative practice is our Welcome Banner, which originally started as a patchwork hanging. However, as people became more involved with the creative process, it seemed a natural progression to suggest that the banner could hang in the entrance foyer and greet people as they came into the building. So it developed into each woman embroidering the word 'welcome' in her first language onto a fragment of fabric, and as these were completed, they were stitched onto a larger piece of material. Since then, we have added to the banner, and it now has the word 'welcome' embroidered in 24 different languages including Luganda, Tajik, Tigrinya, Hungarian, Arabic, Somali and Russian.

As previously discussed, it is important to agree on design decisions when creating a work like this, and we chose a limited range of colours and fabrics, settling on a warm palette of reds, oranges and yellows. Creating an individual element and then placing it within a collaborative work can act as a symbol of acceptance and belonging, and having a limited range of colours gave the banner visual congruency, allowing each woman's contribution to exist harmoniously within the overall design. I led the first iteration of the banner alongside my colleague Sarah Hampson, and when I asked her what she remembered about the process, she said:

> The idea was to involve everyone. One parent always sat quietly watching and listening to the other people in the group. This particular parent was from Latvia and was the only one speaking Russian. She started her patch and people asked her what language she spoke because it had a different alphabet. One person asked her about the stitch she was using and she offered to show her how to do it. Over the weeks she became a strong leader within the group, organising how the banner went together as a whole.

In Branching Out, group members are always encouraged to share their existing skills as well as acquiring new ones (see Figure 7.2). Some of the women lacked confidence with sewing whilst others were old hands and could guide and support them with their work. In the same way, literacy levels vary greatly within the group; one woman, whose mother tongue was Sorani, had not had the opportunity to learn to read or write. Another participant, who was a native Arabic speaker, quietly helped her with the lettering, and when her piece was finished, it felt quite magical that the first word she'd ever written was 'welcome' embroidered in gold.

People were encouraged to share their stories while they worked, and there were detailed discussions of whether you would make tea or coffee to welcome people and how this might be done – either way, offering hot caffeinated drinks

Figure 7.2 Participants working on the banner. Photograph by Luci Gorell Barnes

seemed crucial to the process of hospitality. As this conversation moved around the room, a couple of women sewed a teapot and another small group made a teacup, and these images were sewn onto the banner with embroidered 'tea' pouring from the pot to the cup.

Froggett and Roy (2011) discuss what they call the 'aesthetic third' in which an artwork functions as a shared forum through which ideas can be articulated and understood. As words of welcome were sewn by different hands, the women told stories of home and family, distance and loss, ambitions and disappointments, and the banner acted as our 'aesthetic third', enabling discussions that tend not to happen in more direct encounters. Eszter, one of the participants, commented, 'We got to know each other's country a little bit more as we naturally came up with questions about how you welcome people there, and that generated further conversations'. As we sewed, we stitched our experiences of the world from our different points of view and deepened our understandings of the delicate and complex natures of each other's cultures, for example,

Luci: What would happen if I came to your house?
Rondak: I'd say you're welcome to my house, come and sit down in my sitting room. The women sit down in one room and the men in another, but sometimes they sit together – it's up to you if you don't mind sitting with men.
Luci: I don't mind.
Rondak: Nor do I, but some Kurdish women are shy to sit down with men. I would give you coffee or tea or juice and some nuts. (She gets her phone and finds a photo of mixed nuts including pistachios, cashews and almonds to show me.) But before the nuts I'd give you fresh fruit.
Luci: Like what?
Rondak: Apples, oranges, what I had.

Sometimes I wonder how much of our conversations are evident in the finished artworks and how these exchanges might be captured and relayed to others, or if that would just serve to inhibit future chats. Over the years I have come to the conclusion that rather than trying to 'bottle' our discussions for later, the important thing is to be fully part of them as they emerge. Also, I trust that as we put on our coats and step back out into our different worlds, the seeds of our exchanges travel with us.

5 Reflections

For some of the women, the conversational activity of making the banner was reminiscent of informal pursuits from their countries of origin. For example, Eszter (who is from Hungary) commented:

> When we sat together around the table, sewing and chit chatting it reminded me of my grandma's place. She sometimes got together with her many women neighbours either to help each other with major works on the farm, preparing vegetables for winter, getting things ready for pig killing etc., or in winter to do some sewing or embroidering. The atmosphere felt so relaxed and welcoming.

132 Creating Welcoming Learning Environments

It seems there is a timeless quality about a group of women sat working together, and for many of us, it evoked other female gatherings and shared labours. Writing about their textile-based arts project undertaken with women of diverse religious backgrounds in West London, Dwyer *et al.* observe that:

> The embodied act of sewing together, engaging the material properties of thread and needle, prompted autobiographical storytelling: discussions about learning to sew opened up the sharing of life histories. (Dwyer *et al.*, 2019: 135)

Perhaps it is our familiarity and comfort with this communal, collaborative way of being that prompts us to extend our social bonds through telling stories about our lives.

The combining of many languages into a single artwork gives those who come to the setting a strong sense of the respect and celebration of diversity that underpins our ethos, and the banner has received much positive feedback (see Figure 7.3 and

Figure 7.3 Participant photographing the banner. Photograph by Luci Gorell Barnes

the cover of the book showing the welcome banner). Most importantly, the women themselves are very proud of it, and this sense of achievement is shown in the comments below.

> I really enjoy to do something with my hands. I really like to come here because everyone is very friendly and I love you. I also learn something. My English get better. I learn drawing and painting because I never do something like that at home. When I come here I feel really relaxed.

Filiz Simsek

> I like this group because I want to talk to other people because I want to learn more English. My language is not very good. All day we have activities, we make something with the group. I want to tell other people about my country because my country is very lovely. With the welcome banner I made the teapot and sewed 'welcome' in Badini.

Rondak Mohammed Taher

> I was interested and excited when we made the different languages for 'welcome'. Everyone from different countries used their language. When we finished, I was very excited because we have done a nice job. Every time when I come to the nursery it give me smile to see something nice on the wall. I took some photos to keep. They remind me of what we have done.

Zainab Munye

> My favourite moment happened as soon as we had hung the banner, when one woman took a photo on her phone and immediately sent it to her family and friends in Mogadishu. I felt moved by the idea of our embroidered 'welcomes' winging their way across the world and was reminded how sharing creative practice has the power to connect, enable and inspire us all.

6 Conclusion

Of course, none of us work in isolation and the long-term, ongoing nature of my role at the setting is thanks to the leadership team who have kept me in post despite year on year of savage cuts to services. Such durational relationships are crucial to working with families that we find harder to reach, and the setting's commitment to social inclusion was reflected in our 2014 Ofsted report, which commented:

> Families are made to feel welcome. Differences are respected and celebrated, as seen in the beautiful 'welcome' embroidery in the entrance hall.

Because I am embedded in the staff team, my colleagues have a good understanding of the somewhat oblique nature of my work and are able to make suitable recommendations to the group. I also work with the nursery children, and this allows me to access parents via that role as well. The result is that I have been successful in engaging many of our more socially vulnerable families who might have otherwise slipped quietly through the net. It is a credit to the staff team as a whole that they see the usefulness of this lateral, creative way of working, and how important it is to value women beyond their immediate role as the primary carer of their children.

I would like to end with some feedback written by Howa Suliman, a participant from Darfur, who I worked with for over five years. I've chosen this comment because I feel that as well as addressing issues of cultural integration and improving her English, she also highlights the importance of belonging and connection in the work that the group did together.

> Coming to this group I practice speaking English and meet other women. Speaking sharing new ideas and have fun. It build confidence and I learn new skills and everything good I learn I will reflect it to my family. I make friends and am learning from them or knowing about their cultures. We are more than a group, like becoming a family.

Note

(1) https://www.bristol.gov.uk/documents/20182/32951/Deprivation+in+Bristol+2015/429b2004-eeff-44c5-8044-9e7dcd002faf (accessed on 14 May 2019).

References

Brydon-Miller, M., Greenwood, D. and Maguire, P. (2003) Why action research? *Action Research* 1 (1), 9–28.
Dwyer, C., Beinart, K. and Ahmed, N. (2019) *My Life is but a Weaving*: Embroidering geographies of faith and place. *Cultural Geographies* 26 (1), 133–140.
Freire, P. (1972) *Pedagogy of the Oppressed*. London: Penguin Books.
Froggett, L. and Roy, A. (2011) New Model Visual Arts Organisations & Social Engagement. Unpublished Report. Psychosocial Research Unit, University of Central Lancashire http://www.uclan.ac.uk/schools/school_of_social_work/research/pru/files/wzw_nmi_report.pdf (Accessed July 20th 2012).
Leeson, L. (2018) *Art: Process: Change: Inside a Socially Situated Practice*. New York: Routledge.
Matarasso, F. (2019) *A Restless Art: How Participation Won and Why it Matters*. London: Calouste Gulbenkian Foundation.
Rogers, C.R. (1951) *Client-centered Therapy: Its Current Practice, Implications and Theory*. Boston: Houghton Mifflin.
Watkins, M. (2019) *Mutual Accompaniment and the Creation of the Commons*. New Haven, CT: Yale University Press.
Wicks, P.G., Reason, P. and Bradbury, H. (2008) Living inquiry: Personal, political and philosophical groundings for Action Research Practice. In P. Reason and H. Bradbury (eds) *The SAGE Handbook of Action Research Participative Inquiry and Practice* (pp. 15–30). London: Sage.

8 Creativity, Collaboration and Ways Forward for EAL Learners

Jean Conteh

Two of the things I love about this book are its honesty and its vibrancy. It's a book about creating welcoming learning environments, and the many contributors welcome the reader openly into their classrooms and learning spaces, to show how they work with multilingual learners from the early years to young adults. It's vibrant with their different voices. We hear about teachers, creative practitioners and researchers working together to create the kinds of learning opportunities that we all hope our English as an Additional Language (EAL) learners will experience and enjoy. And there's a sense of unity and common endeavour in it all. As Jane Andrews and Maryam Almohammad outline in their opening chapter, the book is shaped by three guiding principles:

- cooperation and collaboration;
- experiential learning;
- research and classroom practices guided by a 'decolonising ethos' which aim to develop equal, positive relationships among all participants.

The structure of the book gives us space to think about how these principles operate, how ideas become actions and how theories are brought to life in classroom practice. Chapters 3–6 give us frameworks and principles for thinking about working together creatively. The case studies woven between give us vivid examples of the great things that have been happening in multilingual learning settings across the UK. They show how creative collaboration among professionals and the use of different creative media together contribute to constructing a pedagogy that is transformative. They also demonstrate the vital role of research in understanding how it all happens, and in sharing the positive messages that are the outcomes.

In this chapter, I look both backward and forward: backward briefly to the ways that EAL came to be what it is in the system in England and how the ideas in the book fit into our understanding of the importance of creativity, as a broader concept, in teaching and learning. And I look forward to the possibilities for the future, which this book demonstrates. There are three sections: in the first, I reflect on where I think we are at the moment with thinking about 'EAL' in the current social and educational contexts in the UK and what this means for learners, teachers, creative practitioners and researchers. In the second section, I reflect on the idea of creating welcoming learning environments in multilingual classrooms and of what the notion of creativity in teaching and learning can offer to this endeavour, drawing again on ideas and experiences from the past that – for me – speak to the future. Finally, as a teacher educator, I always believed that the 'theory to practice' model was the wrong way round in developing teachers' confidence and skills, so in the final section, I take a 'practice to theory' direction and consider some broad theoretical ideas from the field of language education that I think emerge from and are illustrated by the classroom practices described in the book. I discuss two theoretical perspectives from the broader field of language education – Funds of Knowledge (FoK) and Translanguaging – that, I argue, help us think about the practical principles that can move us forward in our understandings about pedagogy and research in multilingual classrooms.

1 Where Are We Now With EAL?

Over the years, much has been written about the steadily rising numbers in EAL learners in schools in the UK, and the most recent Department for Education statistics (DfE, 2021) – with figures just for England – reflect the well-established trends, though with very slight reductions in some categories, probably as an outcome of the disruptions caused by Covid. They show that, up to June 2021, just less than 1 million pupils in mainstream primary schools in England (about 20%) are recorded as having EAL, along with more than 600,000 pupils in secondary schools (about 17%). The percentage for nurseries is almost 30%, an interesting indicator of future developments. So, by no realistic estimation can it be said that EAL learners are numerically a minority group in schools in England. Indeed, in some parts of the country – as we know – they are actually well into the majority. The accompanying commentary to last year's statistics (DfE, 2020) makes some interesting points about who our EAL learners actually are, today in 21st-century Britain. Reflecting on the increasing numbers over the years, particularly in the early years and primary phases, it states that '… this increase in pupil numbers is largely driven by increases in the birth rate rather than direct current immigration …' (2020: 9). Many (if not most) of the pupils in our nurseries and primary schools who speak other languages besides English, it seems, were born here in this country. So, it's no longer accurate, if it ever was, to say that our EAL learners are from somewhere else; they belong here, they are part of us.

To me, this indicates not just that official statistics always need to be viewed with a critical eye, but that, despite the impression still given by the media and less responsible politicians, migration may not have been the negative force in our schools and society that it is sometimes perceived to be. The population of England has always been diverse, and the nature of this diversity became rapidly much more complex in the first decades of the 21st century, for various reasons (Conteh, 2019: 10–14). Settled British communities of Pakistani, Indian, Bangladeshi, African-Caribbean and other heritage continue to grow. Young people who arrived in the more recent past from all over the world to work and study are now living and working in towns and cities across the country. The superdiversity of our communities, and thus our schools, is becoming simply 'normal'; multilingualism is now just an ordinary part of everyday life. The ways we used to talk about EAL learners, not so long ago, don't mean very much anymore. Many descriptive terms found in policy, especially ones like 'isolated learners' (Conteh, 2019: 10), are becoming more and more meaningless and unhelpful. Perhaps it's time to let go of some of them. Even the label 'EAL' itself may have outlasted its value, its use becoming more and more associated with deficit and disadvantage, rather than success.

Introduced into discourses about language and schooling in England around 20 years ago with the arrival of the National Literacy and Numeracy Strategies, the term 'EAL' was intended to suggest a positive attitude towards the other languages (besides English) spoken by our pupils. But it never quite managed to do that. Hardly surprising, when it was introduced alongside a whole range of descriptive terms and attitudes that implied something was lacking in pupils whose level of English language was not the same as that of 'native speakers'. The first set of standards for teacher training, introduced in 1998, talked about 'pupils not yet fluent in English'. In the same year, the first iteration of the Literacy Strategy had the category of 'pupils in need of support'. In 2000, the National Curriculum introduced the ambivalent concept of 'inclusion' to address issues around particular groups of pupils, such as those who spoke other languages and those with special educational needs. Lots of teachers were led to believe that many of their pupils had somehow been 'excluded' and had to be handled differently from all the others. Safford and Drury (2013) summed it up with their argument that linguistic diversity is inevitably seen as a 'problem' in mainstream education in the UK. They track the history of school provision for multilingual pupils and show how the 'problem' idea became increasingly entrenched in national policies related to curriculum and assessment. And the label of EAL became, in many ways, a shorthand for talking about the 'problem'.

But, perhaps, things are changing, from the grassroots. As this book shows, many teachers are very comfortable with language and cultural diversity and see it as an asset in their classrooms that can enhance their work. The teaching workforce itself is slowly becoming increasingly diverse, bringing greater experience and personal understanding of multilingualism and of living in fluid cultural contexts into our classrooms. But the growing complexity of school populations, especially in the early years, means that all teachers need to be well prepared and supported professionally in their work. However, a recent report (Foley *et al.*, 2018), which provides the most detailed evidence in recent years of the coverage of EAL in initial teacher education in England, shows that both students and tutors feel ill prepared for their roles. The latest official guidance for teacher education (DfE, 2019) does not offer much hope for them. It sets out the core content for initial teacher training, building on the Teachers' Standards that have been in place for almost 10 years. There is no guidance at all for working with multilingual learners – indeed, no mention at all of diversity in any sense, apart from hinting that some learners may have 'additional needs'. Neither is there any new nor specific support for early years practitioners. So it's clear that, in order to be fully prepared for working with EAL learners, teachers and teacher educators will need to do a lot more than depend on the material in the core content document.

Despite this continuing lack of official guidance for teacher training and development, there is a healthy and longstanding tradition of collaborative and creative support for teachers in the field. The National Association for Language Development in the Curriculum (NALDIC) has always been an effective catalyst, and its EAL Journal in Autumn 2019 took teacher development as its theme. Jenny Smith (2019) and Graham Smith (2019) illustrate ways that practitioners who work both inside and outside classrooms can collaborate to improve what happens in multilingual classrooms. Jenny Smith talks about 'action research' (2019: 22), and Graham Smith (2019) discusses partnership or co-teaching. Both point out the importance of building a 'relationship of trust' (2019: 25) among all participants. These are examples of the kinds of collaboration in practice and research that have made a difference in classrooms to the benefit of multilingual learners. In the same vein, De Cat *et al.* (2019: 62) talk about the need for 'two-way exchanges' between teachers and researchers and of the identification of questions 'for the teaching and research communities to address collectively'. No one can question the value of all this, but to make it happen in reality is not always easy. I hope that some of the ideas I discuss in the next sections may be helpful for this.

2 Creating Welcoming Learning Environments – Reflections on Creativity, Collaborative Practice and Research

When I was asked to write this reflective concluding chapter, a Government report on creativity from 1999 sprang to mind. You may not have heard of it, as it has never received the attention it deserved. But it's still available online (DfEE, 1999) and is worth looking at. Led by the inspirational Ken Robinson and using data gathered from a huge range of informants and school settings, the report lays out powerful arguments for the centrality of creativity in learning, not just in what are called the creative arts, but across the whole curriculum. Sadly, Ken Robinson died recently, but he has a strong presence online, and his TED talks (e.g. Robinson, 2007, 2013) are worth watching. In them, he has powerful things to say about creativity. He argues that it's more important in schools than literacy (2007), that it comes about through the interaction of different disciplinary ways of thinking (2013), and is, simply, an essential part of being human. In the wake of the development of standardised testing and the Literacy and Numeracy Strategies, the report had little influence on what happened in schools in the UK in the following years. But it's well worth looking at again today, as we recognise more and more clearly that the education system that has evolved over the past 20 years in England is failing so many of our learners.

The way Robinson's report defines creativity is interesting. It helps us understand the importance of the work presented in this book and also offers some ways of understanding and evaluating the kinds of creative projects that are effective. It identifies four key features of creativity (1999: 28–31) and explains how they relate to a wide range of activities and personal ways of engaging. The first is *imagination*, which is not just fantasising or imaging, but about making fresh or unusual connections through thinking differently. The second feature is *purpose,* which is about the active engagement of an individual in making or producing something. Third is *originality,* which may be in relation to an individual's previous work or to that of their peer group, or to their work in the past. Finally, creativity needs to be of *value* to the task in hand: Imagination, purpose and originality are not enough if they do not lead to an outcome that in some ways is worthwhile on its own terms; the words used in the report to characterise this idea of 'worthwhile' are: 'effective, useful, enjoyable, satisfying, valid or tenable'.

I believe that the last feature is the most important. It encourages us to recognise that the value of a creative activity can't be judged by some kind of external criteria, but by the intrinsic worth of the activity itself, which identifies its worth to those who have created it.

This is amply demonstrated by the authors' conclusions on the creative activities we read about in the book – not one of them describes the outcomes in terms of the participants attaining a particular level in Literacy or Numeracy, or passing a particular exam. Instead, they talk about being 'happy with the result' (of teachers and pupils involved a film project in a primary school), of experiencing 'the pleasure of exploring, creating, sharing and connecting with each other and us as their teachers' (of young migrants involved in a 16+ ESOL programme) and of a parent feeling 'moved and very welcomed' on hearing a familiar song on a school radio station. I could go on quoting the closing comments in virtually every chapter in the book. There is no doubt that the learners did benefit in improving their language, artistic, musical, mathematical and other skills and this was of course valuable. But, to the teachers, creative practitioners and researchers involved in the activities, it was never the main point.

The point was in the intrinsic gains that everyone made, described over and over again in the book in the terms illustrated above, in how the activities made them feel, the sense they gave the participants that they belonged in the classrooms, that their identities were recognised and valued, and that as individuals they mattered. These are the qualities that contribute to the development of confident learners who are empowered in their learning across the whole school curriculum, and able to achieve success.

3 Practice to Theory to Back Again: Thinking About Language, Learning and Identity

In their introductory chapter, Jane Andrews and Maryam Almohammad argue that creative collaboration is vital for promoting creative arts practices in school, and ways of doing this are illustrated in the case studies in the book. They introduce Vera John-Steiner's (2000) ideas about 'creative collaboration', and link them to theoretical ideas about language such as Mercer's 'exploratory talk'. Both John-Steiner and Mercer, in their different ways, are talking about a model of collaboration that goes beyond simply discussing ideas, joint planning and shared working. It's about something more fundamental and transformative. Both see knowledge in the same way, not as an unchanging body of facts and figures, but as a dynamic social entity that can be co-constructed and shared. Mercer (2000) focuses on language, specifically classroom talk, as a means to promote co-reasoning or 'interthinking' and so build a 'thought community'; John-Steiner (2000: 9) talks of the need for 'a shared vision', the construction of which takes time, patience and careful planning. The case studies in the book give many examples of this – you start with an idea and you don't let go until you have a shared understanding of what it means, whether it's embodied in film, as in Chapters 3.1 and 3.2, or printed symbols, as in Chapter 5.1. John-Steiner also argues for the need for 'a chance to be playful as well as critical with each other'. Chapters 5.2, 5.3 and 5.4 all about using music, setting up radio stations, and so on demonstrate this beautifully, showing how an idea can grow and take on a life of its own if it is given the space.

Perhaps most importantly, John-Steiner emphasises the importance of recognising multiple perspectives, of 'establishing equality between partners' (2000: 7). She talks of the need to trust, not just in others, but in yourself. The two are inseparable: 'creative work requires a trust in oneself that is virtually impossible to sustain alone' (2000: 8). We all need recognition from others to maintain our own self-confidence. Most importantly, perhaps, John-Steiner's theories of creative collaboration recognise the social and economic contexts from which the project emerges, as well as the academic ones. Thus, like authors such as Cummins and Early (2011) John-Steiner argues that the identities of all the participants play a crucial role in the processes of teaching, learning and research in which they are engaged. And, as Andrews and Almohammad point out, Cummins and Early's arguments about the need for 'maximum identity investment' in teaching and learning underpin the projects reported in this book.

I think the idea of knowledge as socially constructed rather than as some kind of fixed and absolute artefact is a powerful one, and it's illustrated in the way the case studies are developed. In the rest of this section, I introduce two broad theoretical perspectives from the field of language education that are underpinned by the same idea and are similarly illuminated by the case studies. I introduce them here because I think they are valuable ideas to take forward into future thinking about working creatively in multilingual classrooms and have powerful implications for teaching and learning. Both, essentially, are about identity and empowerment, and how it can be woven into pedagogy. The first, the *Funds of Knowledge* philosophy of teaching and learning, is about linking schools, families and communities, and the second, *Translanguaging*, focuses on linking languages in classrooms.

3.1 Funds of Knowledge

Probably better known in the US than in the UK, the FoK philosophy resonates with many ideas that are familiar to practitioners and researchers in the field of EAL in the UK. It was developed by university-based researchers and teachers working together with Mexican-American families in the southern US (González *et al.*, 2005). Their aim was to transform relationships between schools and communities from ones that were top-down to ones based on mutual empowerment and equality. The university-based researchers wished to change the power relationships among the participants within the research project itself. So they planned and structured their working processes so that they could ' … collaborate with teachers as co-constructors of knowledge rather than solely as consumers of research knowledge' (Rodriguez, 2013: 110).

A central activity in the FoK project was conducting research with families. Moll and his team, along with the teachers, carried out small-scale ethnographic projects with the families of the children they taught. These were developed by the teachers and researchers collaboratively in 'study groups' (González *et al.*, 2005: 17–20), which share similarities with the workshops that Andrews and Almohammad describe in their introduction, which were part of their research.

They were vital sites for the construction of relationships that recognised and valued the different knowledge and power that each participant brought to the projects. A crucial element that emerged through the FoK study groups was reciprocity. Summed up in the Spanish word *confianza*, or 'mutual trust', the teacher-researchers came to recognise that it was a central aspect of the Mexican cultural practices that were woven into the lives of the families. As their understanding of *confianza* grew, the teachers gained insights into the tensions and conflicts that could arise when the children were expected to comply with ways of doing things in school which challenged the values of their homes and communities.

The teachers and researchers in the project argued that, for the pupils, all 'the language and cultural experiences of students' were 'their most important tools for thinking' (Moll, in González *et al.*, 2005: 276). Their main empirical was to 'identify practices that could counteract the negative impact of pervasive cultural deficit views' in schools (Rodriguez, 2013: 89). They believed that teachers needed to understand and build on their pupils' home experiences to promote learning. This may at first glance seem to be a relatively familiar idea.

In UK contexts, terms such as 'activating prior knowledge', 'cultural bridging', 'parental involvement' and so on have for long been used to describe ways of bringing resources from the children's home and community contexts into the classroom. But the FoK philosophy would argue that these approaches are one-way; they are not really about empowering and transforming but are about accessing a fixed curriculum more easily. FoK works to develop two-way conversations. Pupils' and families' relationships with the school are transformed as, at the same time, are teachers' understandings of their pupils and their families.

The approaches in this book show how this aim of seeing things from the children's and their families' perspectives can be achieved in different ways. A wonderful example comes in the work that Luci Gorell Barnes describes in Chapter 7, making a Welcome Banner with a group of parents. Luci's aim was to 'follow the interests and concerns of the group', and she acknowledges that she learns much more from her group than she ever teaches. And in another activity in Chapter 4, Lyn Ma describes very movingly how a FoK approach, embodied in the making of 'identity boxes', contributed to the nurturing of young people, some of whom have suffered the kinds of harrowing experiences that their teachers couldn't possibly have shared, or even imagined. Both bring to life the FoK philosophy, showing how professionals working together with families in creative collaboration can achieve the 'mutual transformation' that González *et al.* (2011: 485) seek to construct.

3.2 Translanguaging

Translanguaging is a way of opening out classrooms to language diversity, and there are many examples of it in the case studies in the book. It affords opportunities for the learner to make links – often in ways that their teachers do not know about – between their experiences outside the classroom and those within. It's about valuing your learners' identities. And, as Blackledge and Creese (2010: 210–215) and many others have argued, identity construction is a vital factor in learning. But it's a common experience among teachers that their learners, particularly older pupils, can be reluctant to use or talk about their home languages in the classroom. Judith Prosser faces this in her secondary school. In Chapter 5.4, she describes how she uses the opportunity of UNESCO's Mother Languages Day to celebrate her pupils' home languages using the school's tannoy system – a delightful example of making voices heard, loud and clear. And in the chapter just before this (5.3), Lois Francis makes an equally engaging case for the value of songs in different languages both to celebrate language and cultural diversity and to open out spaces for multilingual learning.

The theoretical concept of translanguaging is actually very practical, based on the idea that languages together are a holistic resource rather than separate, bounded codes. Cummins' (2001) concepts of the 'common underlying proficiency' (CUP) and linguistic interdependence, ideas well known to EAL practitioners, reflect the same idea, in many ways.

Cummins wanted to stress the positive benefits of transfer in language learning, of the ability of the learner to use their full complement of all the languages they know in their learning of new language, and this is also the essence of translanguaging. Everyone, whether 'multilingual' or 'monolingual', can and does translanguage in a plethora of different ways in their everyday lives in order to do the things they want to do. Young children are particularly adept translanguagers. For the teacher in the classroom, it's about knowing and trusting what your learners can do and giving them the space to develop their own strategies using their own, distinctive range of language resources.

I believe that the ideas coming from FoK and Translanguaging have many practical implications for the ways that teachers and creative practitioners can work collaboratively to develop creative practices in multilingual classrooms. Projects like 'Creating Welcoming Environments' are about theory and practice being brought together in positive and productive ways. The focus of the book is on the outcomes of the projects, on celebrating what happened in the multilingual settings and how it all benefited the learners and their families.

The voices that come through the writing are confident and engaging, sure of the value of what they have achieved. This is testament to the strength of the collaborations developed between the teachers and creative practitioners, clearly built on mutual respect, which allowed the different skills, knowledge and experience brought by each participant to contribute equally to the successful outcomes we read about in the book.

And, without the careful and sensitive engagement of the researchers, all this would not have happened and we would not have known about it. Andrews and Almohammad's third principle was to carry out research guided by a 'decolonising ethos', developing equal, positive relationships among all the participants. This book is proof of their success. They sought to understand the questions they posed about how to create welcoming environments for multilingual learners through engaging with the practical contexts and then endeavouring to better understand them and support their development. Their work is at the centre of a new way of thinking about the links between theory and practice, and between research and practice that will make the differences we all aspire to for our multilingual learners.

References

Blackledge, A. and Creese, A. (2010) *Multilingualism: Critical Perspectives*. London: Continuum.
Conteh, J. (2019) *The EAL Teaching Book: Promoting Success for Multilingual Learners* (3rd edn). London: Learning Matters/Sage.
Cummins, J. (2001) *Negotiating Identities: Education for Empowerment in a Diverse Society* (2nd edn). Ontario, CA: CABE/Trentham.
Cummins, J. and Early, M. (eds) (2011) *Identity Texts: The Collaborative Creation of Power in Multilingual Schools*. London: Trentham Books.
De Cat, C., Oxley, E. and Sadig, H. (2019) Guiding questions to inform CPD. *EAL Journal* Autumn 2019, 59–62.
DfE (2019) *Initial Teacher Training Core Content Framework*. DfE-00230-2019. See https://assets.publishing.service.gov.uk/government/uploads/system/uploads/attachment_data/file/843676/Initial_teacher_training_core_content_framework.pdf (accessed February 2022).
DfE (2020) *Schools, Pupils and their Characteristics, Academic Year 2019–2020*. See https://explore-education-statistics.service.gov.uk/find-statistics/schoolpupils-and-their-characteristics (accessed September 2020).
DfE (2021) *Schools, Pupils and Their Characteristics (Main Text), June 2021*. See https://explore-education-statistics.service.gov.uk/find-statistics/school-pupils-and-their-characteristics (accessed February 2022).
DfEE (1999) *All Our Futures: Creativity, Culture and Education*. See http://sirkenrobinson.com/pdf/allourfutures.pdf (accessed February 2022).
Foley, Y., Anderson, C., Conteh, J. and Hancock, J. (2018) *Initial Teacher Education and English as an Additional Language*. Cambridge: The Bell Foundation/The University of Edinburgh.
González, N., Moll, L. and Amanti, C. (eds) (2005) *Funds of Knowledge: Theorizing Practices in Households, Communities and Classrooms*. New York: Routledge.
González, N., Wyman, L. and O'Connor, B. (2011) The past, present and future of "Funds of Knowledge". In M. Pollock and B. Levinson (eds) *A Companion to the Anthropology of Education* (pp. 481–494). Malden. MA: Wiley-Blackwell.
John-Steiner, V. (2000) *Creative Collaboration*. Oxford: Oxford University Press.
Mercer, N. (2000) *Words and Minds*. London: Routledge.
Moll, L. (2005) Reflections and possibilities. In N. González, L. Moll and C. Amanti (eds) *Funds of Knowledge: Theorizing Practices in Households, Communities and Classrooms* (pp. 275–287). New York: Routledge.
Robinson, K. (2007) *Do Schools Kill Creativity?* See https://www.youtube.com/watchv=iG9CE55wbtY (accessed February 2022).
Robinson, K. (2013) *How to Escape Education's Death Valley*. See https://www.youtube.com/watch?v=wX78iKhInsc (accessed February 2022).
Rodriguez, G.M. (2013) Power and agency in education: Exploring the pedagogical dimensions of Funds of Knowledge. *Review of Research in Education* 37, 87–120.
Safford, K. and Drury, R. (2013) The 'problem' of bilingual settings: Policy and research in England. *Language and Education* 27 (1), 70–81.
Smith, G. (2019) CPD: What, where, who and how? *EAL Journal* Autumn 2019, 24–26.
Smith, J. (2019) EAL teacher training: What works well and what is needed? *EAL Journal* Autumn 2019, 59–62.

Afterword: Summary of Ideas for Practice

Jane Andrews and Maryam Almohammad

- Creative projects can bring to life the languages of the school or college community and thereby shed light on linguistic diversity which may not be fully appreciated otherwise.
- Crafting activities can provide opportunities for learners to share aspects of their lives, languages and interests while also opening up speaking and listening opportunities in language-rich classrooms.
- Displays crafted in the school or college can do a great job of engaging learners, parents and teachers in linguistic diversity – more so than commercially produced posters showing a selection of ways of saying 'hello' in different languages which may not represent the actual languages used in the school or college.
- Activities that engage learners with art forms (visual, music) can open up interests and interactions with learners, parents and teachers and generate a welcoming learning environment.
- Participation in creative approaches does not require artistic expertise (on the part of learners or teachers); however, creative projects are an ideal opportunity for building collaborations with artists in our communities to inspire and enhance our learning and teaching.
- Performing and making announcements allow us to experiment with our voices and languages all of which are valuable for language learning and also for developing self-esteem and a sense of achievement.
- Tangible products such as printed artefacts or an embroidered banner allow individuals to express themselves and for the products to be displayed, shared and enjoyed by the community in the educational setting.

Index

Note: References in *italics* are to figures, those in **bold** to tables; 'n' refers to chapter notes.

16+ ESOL Programme *see* creative arts in ESOL classroom

action research 129, 138
activities 3–4
Adinkra creative links 8, 68–70
   Adinkra textile printing 78, *78*, 79
   artistic hospitality 73–74
   co-creation: music 75–77
   methodology and process 74–75, *75*
   pedagogy of welcome 73–74
   treasured opportunities 72–73
   conclusion 79–81
Adinkra symbols 68, 69, 76, 77
   rationale and context 70–72, *71*
Adinkra symbols and printing 8, 83–86, *86*
   activity 84
   context 83
   how it went 84–85
   my reflections 85–86
   our school display *85*
   rationale 83–84
'aesthetic third' 131
afterword: summary of ideas for practice 8–9, 144
AHRC Community Filmmaking and Cultural Diversity Project 24–25
AHRC Connected Communities Project
   filmmaking on language inequality and power 30, *31*
   funding 25
   imagineering and community filmmaking 31–33
   'Language as Talisman' *32*, 32–33
Almohammad, M. 1–9, 23–33, 36, 139, 144
Anderson, J. *et al.* 26, 27, 30, 144
Andrews, J. *et al.* 1–9, 36, 98–113, 139
Anyidoho, K. 19
Aotearoa, New Zealand 16
arts

   in education 104–105
   and languages 105–106, 112–113
Arts and Humanities Research Council 13–14
audio in school 95–97, *96*

background to the book 4–6
Bellsham-Revell, A. 4
belonging 47
Bishopp, S. 36
Blackledge, A. 142
Blaise High School, Bristol, UK 62–64
Bloom, S.L. 14
British Educational Reserarch Association Ethical Guidelines 7
British Film Institute (BFI) 26
British Sign Language (BSL) 37, 39–40
Brueggemann, W. 14, 16
Brydon-Miller, M. *et al.* 129

Canagarajah, S. 24
children's needs and preferences *see* creative techniques: children's needs and preferences
China–Burkina Faso migration *see* South-South Migration Hub
China–Ghana migration *see* South-South Migration Hub
China–Ivory Coast migration *see* South-South Migration Hub
Christchurch Church of England Primary School, Hanham, Bristol, UK 36–37
circles 111–112
class level activities 4
co-operation and collaboration 3, 5, 6, 32, 50, 79, 103–104, 135
   see also 'Welcome Banner': cultural exchange
co-operative professional development (CPD) 5–6
co-teaching 138

cohesion building in school through crafting 8, 65–67
collaboratioin 103–104
Comfort, Anna 8, 114–120
common underlying proficiency (CUP) 142
community filmmaking 7–8, 23–25
　AHRC Community Filmmaking and Cultural Diversity Project 24–25
　AHRC Connected Communities Project 25, 30–33
　creating filming with children and young people 25–30
　participatory community filmmaking 25
　why multilingual filming? 26
complex learning difficulties *see* creative techniques: children's needs and preferences
Connery, C. *et al.* 3
Conteh, Jean 8, 135–143
Cope, B. 23, 24
Cornell, Joseph 2, 54, *54*
Cox, S. 17, 18
CPD (co-operative professional development) 5–6
crafting 5, 65–67
creative arts approaches
　breadth of EAL teachers' work 4
　creative collaboration 3
　reason for 1–4
creative arts in ESOL classroom: creative arts activities 50
　identity boxes 2, *54*, 54–56, *55*, *56*, 141
　murals 50–51, *51*
　self-portraits 51, *52*
　suitcases 52–53, *54*, 59–60, 62–64, *63*
　conclusion 56–57
creative arts in ESOL classroom: introduction and context 8, 42, *43*
　16+ ESOL Programme 42–43
　funding 44
　programme content 45–46
　programme rationale 44–45
　referral process 45
　students 44
creative arts in ESOL classroom: overall approach 46
　16+ ESOL curriculum 48–49
　being nurtured 48
　belonging 47
　building resilience 47–48
　challenges and barriers to learning 49
　creative arts activities 50
　why include creative arts? 49–50
　working together 46
creative arts processes for EAL children
　drama games 119–120
　'The Magic Hat' project 114
　'The Magic Shoes' project 114–115
　work scheme 116–118
creative techniques: assessing children's language 8, 62–64
creative techniques: children's needs and preferences 554
　background to the school 58
　pedagogic approach 58–59
　suitcase activity 52–53, *54*, 59–60, 62–64, *63*
　what next? 60–61
creativity 17, 138–139
creativity, collaboration and ways forward 8, 135–136
　creating welcoming learning environments 138–139
　Funds of Knowledge (FoK) 136, 140–141
　practice, theory: language, learning and identity 139–143
　translanguaging 142–143
　where are we now with EAL? 136–138
Creese, A, 142
'Critical Connections: Multilingual Digital Storytelling' project 25, 26–30
　digital storytelling during COVID pandemic 30
　'Our Planet Festival' 30, *31*
cultural heritage 2
Culverhill School, Yate, Bristol, UK 58–61
Cummins, J. 2, 3–4, 23, 139, 142
CUP (common underlying proficiency) 142
CWLE project (Creating Welcoming Learning Environments: Disseminating Arts-Based Approaches to Including all Learners) 4–7, *7*

dance and movement 108–109
De Cat, C. *et al.* 138
Deaf Awareness Week 37
deaf children *see* filmmaking project
decolonising ethos 5, 6, 17–18, 135, 142–143
'decolonization of "helping" professionals' 127
Demie, F. 2–3

digital storytelling *see* 'Critical Connections: Multilingual Digital Storytelling' project
drama games 119–120
drums 93, 100–101
Drury, R. 137
Dwyer, C. *et al.* 132

Eagleton, T. 17
EAL *see* English as an Additional Language
Early, M. 2, 23, 142
early years settings: songs from Jamaica 91–94
East Bristol Children's Centres (EBCC) 125–126
Edge, J. 5
Egypt-Jordan migration *see* South-South Migration Hub
Elmfield School for Deaf Children, Hanham, Bristol, UK 38–40
EMAS (Portsmouth Ethnic Minority Achievement Service) 65–67
English as a foreign language 24
English as an Additional Language (EAL) 12–13, 26, 135
　audio in school 95–97, *96*
　building cohesion through crafting 8, 65–67
　celebration through film 36–37
　class level activities 4
　and complex learning difficulties 58
　coordinators 4
　creative arts approaches 1–4
　creative arts processes 114–120
　filmmaking project 38–40
　GCSE English: first languages poetry 121–124
　one-to-one level activities 4
　teachers' work 4
　were are we now? 136–138
　whole school activities 4
'English last' 18
Escott, H. 30, 31–33
ESOL (English for Speakers of Other Languages) *see* creative arts in ESOL classroom
Essel, O. 69
Ethnic Minority and Traveller Achievement Service, South Gloucestershire, UK
　Jamaican songs 91–94
　school radio station 87–90
exiled speech 16–17

experiential learning 5, 6, 135
'exploratory talk' 3–4

faith 59
Fassetta, G. *et al.* 15
Fay, R. *et al.* 74
filming with children and young people 7–8, 25–26
　AHRC Connected Communities Project 30–33
　celebration through film 36–37
　'Critical Connections: Multilingual Digital Storytelling' project 25, 26–30
　multilingual/multicultural digital storytelling films 27–30
　why multilingual filming? 26
　conclusion 33
filmmaking project
　introduction and rationale 38
　planning, delivery, resources 38–40
　conclusion 40
　see also community filmmaking
Foley, Y. *et al.* 137
Francis, Lois 8, 91–94, 142
Freire, P. 129
French as a foreign language 24
Frimberger, K. *et al.* 2, 5, 14, 28, 36
Froggett, L. 131
Funds of Knowledge (FoK) 136, 140–141

Gadamer, Hans-Georg 81n3
Ganyamatope *see* Sitholé, Tawona
GCSE English: first languages poetry
　'A Funeral' 122–123
　English as an Additional Language 121–122
　'The Dusty Foot Philosopher' 123–124
gerunds 10–12, 11*f*
Ghana *see* Adinkra symbols
GIRFEC (Getting it right for every child) 46
Glasgow Clyde College 42–57
González, N. *et al.* 140, 141
Gorell Barnes, Luci 8, 125–134, 141
Grant, D. 38
Grotzke, Alison 8, 83–86
guiding principles 5, 135

Haiti–Brazil migration *see* South-South Migration Hub
Hampson, Sarah 130
hermeneutics 70, 81n3

Herrero, C. 24
Hiorns, Lydia 12 73
Holzman, L. 3

ideas for practice, summary of 144
identity boxes 2, *54*, 54–56, *55*, *56*, 141
identity construction 142
Identity Suitcases 65–67
identity texts 2, 23–24
imagination 138, 139
Improvement Hub of Education Scotland 44
inclusive curriculum 2–3, 137
Ingold, T. 12, 17, 18
intercultural language education 23

Jamaican songs 91–94
John Muir Conservation Award 45, 47
John-Steiner, V. 3, 139–140

Kalantzis, M. 23
K'naan: 'The Dusty Foot Philosopher' 123–124
knowledge 12, 17, 19, 129
    Funds of Knowledge 136, 140–141
    in home and community 26, 28
    as socially constructed 139–140
Kolb, D.A. 6
Kramsch, C. 16–17

language 12
language assessment using creative techniques 8, 62–64
languages
    and arts 105–106, 112–113
    on the tannoy system 95–97, *96*
learning environments 4–7, 138–139
Leavy, Patricia 69–70
Leeson 18 128
Lewis, K. 2–3
Lievaart, Alicja 8, 38–40
linguistic interdependence 142
literacy: sensory literacy 28
Literacy Strategy 137
Lobb, Richard 114

Ma, Lyn 5, 8, 42–57, 62, 141
Macleroy, V. 26, 28–30, *29*
'Magic Hat' project 114
'Magic Shoes' project 114–115
Malaysia–Nepal migration *see* South-South Migration Hub

Malik, S. *et al*. 24–25
Māori community 6
Matarasso, F. 127, 128
Matthews, Catherine 114
Menon, E. 38
Mercer, N. 3, 139
MIDEQ (Migration for Development and Equality) *see* South-South Migration Hub
Miltoncross Academy, Portsmouth, UK 65–67
Moll, M. 141
monolingual language policies 23
Moore, Dominique 8, 87–90, 121–124
Multilingual Digital Storytelling Awards (2016) 27
multilingual education 23
multilingual filming 26
multilingual/multicultural digital storytelling films 27–30
multilingualism 4–5
multiliteracies 23, 24
Munye, Zainab 133
murals 50–51, *51*
music 5, 8
    Adinkra Creative Links 75–77
    Jamaican songs 91–94
    school radio station 87–90

NALDIC (National Association for Language Development in the Curriculum) 4, 8, 138
Nancarrow, P. 4
National Curriculum 137
National Resource Centre for Supplementary Education 26
Newland, M. 1, 3
Nutbrown, C. 1

one-to-one level activities 4
Opoku-Mensah, I. 69
originality 138–139
Orwin, Dr Martin 123
'Our Planet Festival' 30, *31*

Pahl, K. 23, 30, 31–33
partnership 138
Paul Hamlyn Foundation 25, 26, 44
Pelias, R.J. 70
phenomenology 70
Phipps, Alison 5, 7, 8, 10–20, 75, 98, 99
plays 8

plurilingual repertoires 28
poetry 5, 8, 17–18, 103–104, 121–124
Polish poems 122–123
Portsmouth Ethnic Minority Achievement Service (EMAS) 65–67
practice to theory 136
present participles 10
Prosser, Judith 8, 62–64, 95–97, 142
purpose 138, 139

Reeve, Rebecca 8, 65–67
research 6
resilience 47–48
RM@Borders (Researching Multilingually at the Borders of the Law, Language, the Body and the State) 4–5
Robinson, K. 138
Rodriguez, G.M. 141
Rogers, C.R. 128
Rowsell, J. 23
Roy, A. 131
Rubens, M. 1, 3

Safford, K. 137
Salcedo, Doris 129
Sanctuary Model 14
Santos, B.d.S. 17
school for deaf children *see* filmmaking project
school languages on the tannoy system 95–97, 142
school radio station 87–90
Scotland *see* Adinkra creative links; creative arts in ESOL classroom
Scottish Refugee Council 36
sculpture 27, 102–103
Seasons for Growth programme 48
sedimented identities 23
self-portraits 51, 52
sensory literacy 28
SHANARRI (Safe, Healthy, Achieving, Nurtured, Active, Respected, Responsible and Included) 46
Sharland, Gemma 7–8, 36–37
Simsek, Filiz 133
Sitholé, Tawona: a conversation 5, 8, 98–113
  arts and languages 105–106, 112–113
  arts in education 104–105
  circles 111–112
  collaboration 103–104
  dance and movement 108–109
  drums 100–101

inspiration 98, 110–111
objects 106–107
poets in school 103–104
sculpture 102–103
South-South Migration Hub (MIDEQ) 98–113
stories 101–102
translating 109–110
working with groups 102
Smith, Graham 138
Smith, Jenny 138
Somali poems 123–124
South Africa–Ethiopia migration *see* South-South Migration Hub
South-South Migration Hub (MIDEQ) 98–113
Spanish as a foreign language 24
speaking skills 62–64
Speedwell Children's Centre, East Bristol 125
  Branching Out *126*, 126–134
spoken word 8, 26
St Michael's on the Mount Primary School, Bristol, UK 114–120
Storey, J. 81n3
stories and storytelling 25, 26–30, 101–102
structure of the book 6, 7–9
'suitcase' activity 52–53, *54*, 59–60, 62–64, *63*
Suliman, Howa 134
Szymborska, Wislawa: 'A Funeral' 122–123

Taher, Rondak Mohammed 133
tannoy system 95–97, 142
teacher education 137
Teachers' Standards 137
textile printing 5, 78, *78*, *79*, 83–86, *85*
'theory to practice' 136
Thomas, Karen 8, 65–67
Tippett, Su 8, 58–61
Tordzro, Gameli 8, 68–81, 99
Tordzro, Naa Densua 5, 8, 68–81, 99
transition ceremonies 15–16
translanguaging 28, 40, 136, 142–143
translating 109–110
Translating Cultures Theme 25
translingual practice 24
treasured opportunities 72–73
trust 3, 45, 138
Tuhiwai Smith, L. 6

UASC (Unaccompanied Asylum-Seeking Children) *see* creative arts in ESOL classroom

unaccompanied minors 8, 42–43
   see also creative arts in ESOL classroom: introduction and context
UNESCO: Mother Languages Day 95, 142
University of Glasgow Hunterian Museum 69
University of Stirling 44

value 139
Vanderschelden, I. 24
Vass, E. *et al.* 74
'visual poetry' 5

Watkins, Mary 127
ways forward *see* creativity, collaboration and ways forward
'Welcome Banner': cultural exchange 8, 125, *132*, 141
   context 125–127
   making the Welcome Banner 129–131, *130*
   process 127–129
   reflections 131–133
   conclusions 133–134
welcoming learning environments 138–139
well in welcoming, the 7, 10
   crafting, making, finding the poetry 17–19
   hardest thing about learning English is 12–13
   hospitable parts of speech 10–12
   transition ceremonies of welcome and arrival 15–16
   welcoming exiled speech 16–17
   Well 19–20
   well in welcome, the 13–15
Wheatfield Primary School, Bradley Stoke, Bristol, UK 83–86
Wicks, P.G. *et al.* 129

zone of proximal development (ZPD) 3